What People Are Saying About
The Climb of Your Life ...

"If you are in dire need of a paradigm shift, a rush of hope and a panoramic view for your intellect and spirit, look no further than *The Climb of Your Life*. Metaphor is the most powerful tool in language, and Mark Atteberry has summitted King David's mountain-climbing metaphor with remarkable grace and muscle. A delight-driven adventure awaits. Rope in and follow his lead."

—**Donald Miller**
author, *Blue Like Jazz*

"Mark Atteberry has written a terrific book about the Christian life. There's no theological jargon here, just plain talk about the call to higher ground that is issued to every Christian. *The Climb of Your Life* is filled with Scripture, humor, inspiring stories and practical application. The discussion questions at the end will make it a favorite of Bible school classes and home study groups."

—**Ben Merold**
senior pastor, Harvester Christian Church

THE CLIMB OF YOUR LIFE

FINDING YOUR HOME
ON THE
MOUNTAIN OF THE LORD

MARK ATTEBERRY

Deerfield Beach, Florida
www.faithcombooks.com

Library of Congress Cataloging-in-Publication Data
is available from the Library of Congress.

©2004 Mark Atteberry
ISBN 0-7573-0199-1

Faith Communications (FC), its Logos and Marks are trademarks of Health Communications, Inc.

Publisher: Faith Communications
          An Imprint of Health Communications, Inc.
          3201 S.W. 15th Street
          Deerfield Beach, Florida 33442-8190

Cover and inside book design by Lawna Patterson Oldfield
Cover photo ©Fotosearch

FOR MY DAUGHTER, MICHELLE

TWENTY-SIX YEARS AGO I CRADLED YOU IN MY ARMS
AND LOOKED INTO YOUR LITTLE BLUE EYES
AND WONDERED WHAT YOU WOULD BECOME

TODAY I STAND IN AWE
YOU HAVE FAR EXCEEDED MY EVERY DREAM
I LOVE YOU

Other books by Mark Atteberry

The Samson Syndrome

The Caleb Quest

Contents

Acknowledgments

A time-honored adage says, "If you see a turtle sitting on a fence post, you know he had some help." As this, my third book, hits the shelves, I feel like that turtle. I have been helped by some wonderful people. Among them are:

My wife, Marilyn, and my daughter, Michelle, who fill my life with joy.

My friend, Pat Williams, of the Orlando Magic, who instantly caught the vision of this book.

My agent, Lee Hough, who represents me with unshakable integrity and has become a trusted friend.

My editors, Susan Heim, who made my first Faith Communications experience a wonderful one, and Genene Hirschhorn.

My flock, the members and friends of Poinciana Christian Church, who treat me the way every pastor would love to be treated.

And last, but not least, my friend and favorite author, Karen Kingsbury, who, more than anyone else, is responsible for my writing career.

Introduction

You've just opened a unique book about the Christian life. I realize that's a bold claim, especially since you probably found it tucked in among hundreds of others on your bookstore shelf. But I believe it's a valid claim for one simple reason: It offers a picture of the Christian life that has seldom been seen.

The common approach is to picture the Christian life as a fight (2 Tim. 4:7), a walk (Micah 6:8) or a race (Heb. 12:1). These are meaningful images to be sure, and many wonderful sermons and books have made them come alive in our minds. But the Bible contains another striking picture of the Christian life that has been largely overlooked. It was painted by David in Psalm 24:3–6:

> Who may climb the mountain of the Lord?
> Who may stand in his holy place?
> Only those whose hands and hearts are pure
> Who do not worship idols
> And never tell lies.
> They will receive the Lord's blessing

And have right standing with God their savior.
They alone may enter God's presence
And worship the God of Israel.

David says that living for the Lord is like climbing a mountain.

It's a passion for the hill country.

A wrestling match with gravity.

A constant struggle for altitude.

One reason this fascinating image has received so little attention is because it comes from an Old Testament passage, and we generally turn to the New Testament when studying the Christian life. A second reason is because it sits in the shadow of Psalm 23, arguably the most beloved chapter in the Bible. Psalm 24 is like the kid sister of a gorgeous movie star ... beautiful in its own right, but few people ever notice.

But just as the Bible is no less the Word of God simply because it's sitting on a shelf collecting dust, so this picture of the life of faith is no less a masterpiece just because it's been long overlooked. My purpose in this book is to carry David's painting down from the attic, dust it off and hang it on the wall for everyone to see.

And boy, do we need to see it.

Having been a pastor for almost thirty years, I know that our churches are full of valley dwellers ... people who have never reached their potential, never overcome their besetting sins and never experienced God's richest blessings. Every

Sunday in churches all across America you'll find them wearing artificial smiles and robotically going through the motions of worship, yet feeling defeated and discouraged on the inside. Their faith has grown stale, they've lost the enthusiasm they started out with, and what's worse, they have no idea what to do about it.

Maybe you're one of those people.

Maybe you've been a Christian for a while, but have not made the kind of progress toward maturity that you were hoping for or that others around you have made. Perhaps you're still struggling with the same old destructive habits and attitudes that used to plague you before you accepted Christ. Maybe you've made several honest efforts to get your act together, but for some reason you always seem to lose the ground you gain and then some. And maybe now your frustration has grown to the point that you've even thought about chucking the whole "Christian thing" altogether.

Well, my friend, Psalm 24:3–6 could hold the answer you're looking for.

David's mountain of the Lord passage pulls no punches as it calls you to higher ground. It implores you to turn your sad little life into a great big adventure. It offers you the chance to break out of your monotonous routine and try something risky for a change. It challenges you to travel to a place where many people never go—where many people are *afraid* to go— but where priceless, eternal, life-changing treasures are waiting to be discovered.

The good news is that you don't have to be an experienced climber to tackle the mountain of the Lord. Even if you've never climbed anything higher than the stepladder in your garage . . . even if K2 sounds to you like the formula for an all-purpose bathroom cleaner . . . even if the only Rockies you know anything about play baseball in the Western Division of the National League, you don't need to be intimidated. This is a skill you can learn. Even the world's greatest mountaineers started with an instructor and a single step.

I have included nine chapters in this book, and each one discusses in very practical terms a step you must take if you want to discover the rich treasures that can only be found on the mountain of the Lord. You may find some of the steps to be more difficult than others, but none of them are out of reach if you're really serious about changing the direction of your life. In fact, the steps are arranged in such a way that each one prepares you for the one to follow, so that you get stronger as you go. I've also filled the book with the dramatic stories of real-life climbers and quotes from some of the world's greatest mountaineers to encourage and inspire you to new heights.

I don't know how you came to hold this book in your hands at this moment. Maybe the jacket design caught your eye. Maybe it was given to you by a friend. Or maybe the year is 2010, and you found this moldy, dog-eared copy on a thrift-store shelf. However it happened, I'd like for you to at least consider the possibility that you're holding this book because

God willed it. Maybe this is His way of reaching out to you ... of showing you that your life really could change for the better ... that there are blessings and treasures beyond your wildest dreams that are waiting to be discovered. Maybe this book is God's invitation for you to meet Him on the mountain so He can show you what you've been missing.

Right now, would you give just about anything to get out of the rut you're in?

If so, then my friend, it's time to climb!

Turn the page and let's go.

David will show us the way.

Part One:

THE PREPARATION

I am resolved no longer to linger
Charmed by the world's delight
Things that are higher
Things that are nobler
These have allured my sight

Palmer Hartsough and James H. Fillmore,
"I Am Resolved," 1896

One

LIFT UP YOUR EYES

*"As a mountain climber,
I've always felt more drawn to the top
than driven from the bottom."*

—David Breashears

Why do people climb?

If you've ever seen a rock climber hanging by his fingers and toes from a two-hundred-foot cliff, you've surely asked that question. The legendary mountaineer, George Mallory, who disappeared without a trace on Mt. Everest in 1924 (only to be found frozen on the mountain in 1999), once was asked why he was so determined to stand atop the world's highest peak. "Because it's there," he said.

But we all know there had to be more to it than that. Perhaps Mallory was in no mood to talk about his motivation at that moment, or maybe he found words inadequate to express it. Either way, most people believe there was a more substantive reason that he devoted his life to something so dangerous and demanding.

I believe the motivations that drive people to climb are not as numerous or as complicated as many people think. Let me illustrate by telling you about an old tomcat that used to hang out in our neighborhood.

He could climb a tree as easily as I can climb a flight of stairs, but I only saw ol' Tom scamper up the oak in our front yard on two occasions. One was when an ill-tempered dog from down the street seemed determined to separate Tom's head from the rest of his body. The other was when he spotted his lunch (a bird) sitting on a limb. In the former situation, Tom was being *driven* up the tree. In the latter, he was being *drawn* up the tree. And so it is that all climbing boils down to these two motivations.

We're either driven or we're drawn.

We're either trying to escape something or we're trying to embrace something.

When it comes to the mountain of the Lord, some people would say that it doesn't matter why you climb, just so you climb. That sounds good, and it may be true that any motivation is better than no motivation. But clearly, it's better to be drawn than driven.

People who come running to the mountain of the Lord with problems nipping at their heels often disappear as soon as the problems do, just as ol' Tom would come slinking down the tree as soon as the neighbor's ill-tempered dog had wandered off down the street. But people who are drawn to the mountain of the Lord because of the unique treasures it has to offer rarely give up their quest. For them, the climbing experience often becomes a lifelong passion as each new discovery holds the promise of something even more wonderful just over the next ridge.

In Scripture, Caleb is a striking example of a drawn climber. When he was forty, Moses promised to give him the hill country of Hebron (Num. 14:24). Unfortunately, the nation's sin resulted in a forty-year detour through the wilderness, and all of Caleb's dreams had to be put on hold. But he never forgot Moses' promise. For forty-five years he lived with his heart set on those hills, longing to climb and conquer. Finally, at the age of eighty-five and with the wilderness behind him, Caleb could contain his passion no longer. He approached his friend, Joshua, and stated his case:

*N*ow, *as you can see, the Lord has kept me alive and well as He promised for all these forty-five years since Moses made this promise—even while Israel wandered in the wilderness. Today I am eighty-five years old. I am as strong now as I was when Moses sent me on that journey, and I can still travel and fight as well as I could then. So I'm asking you* *to* give me the hill country *that the Lord promised me. You will remember that as scouts we found the Anakites living there in great, walled cities. But if the Lord is with me, I will drive them out of the land, just as the Lord said. (Josh. 14:10– 12, author's emphasis)*

You can sense the emotion in Caleb's words. He was being drawn to those hills so powerfully that not even his advanced age or the dreaded Anakites could dampen his enthusiasm. It's no surprise, then, that Joshua granted his request. Nor is it a surprise that Caleb fully accomplished his dream. Joshua 14:14 says it all: "Hebron therefore became the inheritance of Caleb."

My friend, if you have come to the mountain of the Lord seeking an avenue of escape from the problems that are hounding you, I'm glad. Know that you have made a good choice. The Scriptures teach that there is no greater refuge you could seek (Ps. 61:1–3). But know as well that the road that stretches upward before you is more than just a way out. It's a way *in*—a way into the life you've always wanted.

Lift up your eyes and catch a glimpse of just a few of the treasures that await you.

Treasure #1: People

The first thing you'll notice about the mountain of the Lord is that it's humming with activity. Unlike the panoramic photos you've seen of Mt. Everest, which look so lonely and desolate, the mountain of the Lord actually is quite busy. Millions of people are climbing already, and countless newcomers are joining them every day.

You'll also notice that those who have chosen to climb the mountain of the Lord fit no particular stereotype. Every shape, size, age, nationality and personality type will be represented. Some will be experienced spiritual mountaineers, and others will be novices taking their first hesitant steps in the faith. Some will have been driven to the mountain of the Lord by devils, and others will have been drawn by dreams. But the one thing they'll share is an aptitude for altitude, a desire to leave the valley behind.

Of course, some people will want to climb solo, but it's clear that our Lord intends for us to climb in groups. The Bible contains countless directives regarding the importance of counsel, encouragement, sharing and teamwork. And Jesus emphatically confirmed the importance of climbing together when he chose not one person, but twelve people, to be his disciples and carry on his work.

I'll dig deeper into this thought in chapter 3, but for now let me just say that the relationships I've built with my fellow climbers on the mountain of the Lord are some of my most cherished treasures. The people I have met on the slopes are some of the best people in the world. They're not perfect by any means, but they are different in many ways from those who are content to live in the valley. They are generally more pleasant, more positive, more compassionate, more trustworthy and more dependable. I couldn't begin to count the number of times I've been helped along and brought closer to the summit by a fellow climber who, at that moment, was just a little stronger or more courageous than I was. If I had been climbing alone, I never would have made it this far.

TREASURE #2: PERSPECTIVE

Have you ever noticed how even a slight change in altitude can make a dramatic change in the way things look? Try watching a football game from ground level. It looks like mass chaos. But if you climb up a few dozen rows in the stadium, suddenly the various aspects of the game become apparent. You can see blocking schemes and pass patterns develop. You can see holes open (and close), and infractions occur. You can understand why the ball carrier dashes to the right or left, and why the official tosses his yellow hanky. Well, *sometimes* you can understand why the official tosses his yellow hanky!

Life is like a football game in that it's better viewed from higher elevations. As you gain altitude on the mountain of the Lord, you begin to see things differently.

Michael Andriano is an outstanding young preacher who started and is leading the highly successful River Run Christian Church in Orlando. I first met Mike in 1990 when he and his wife, Linda, walked into Poinciana Christian Church, cold turkey. They were as sweet as they could be, but very worldly and clueless about the ways of God. However, they were honestly seeking the truth, and it soon became my privilege to baptize them into Christ.

Just before he was baptized, Mike told me that he intended to keep enjoying an occasional beer or glass of wine, as had been his practice for years. He squared up his shoulders and said, "I believe it's okay as long as I don't get drunk." I didn't argue. I simply said what I always say: "That's fine. Just promise me you'll pray about it and keep an open mind. The Lord may lead you to a different conclusion."

Less than three months later, Mike confessed to me that he had quit drinking altogether. I couldn't help smiling and asked him why. He said, "I don't know. Things just look different to me now." The reason things looked different was because he'd been climbing for a while. He'd gained some altitude, and with it came a fresh new perspective.

Dear reader, let me make you this promise: You're going to like the way life looks from the mountain. All of your old problems still will be there in plain sight, but from a higher elevation they'll look smaller and more manageable. Plus— and this is so important—from a higher elevation you'll be able to see *beyond* your problems. You'll be able to see what's often called "the big picture." It's the way life looks when you get the panoramic view, when you take *everything* into consideration, not just the problem at hand. Paul, who reached great heights on the mountain of the Lord, was looking at the big picture when he said, "What we suffer now is nothing compared to the glory He will give us later" (Rom. 8:18).

If you are a person who always has struggled with a dark outlook on life, you of all people should be excited about making this climb. You should be longing for a fresh point of view.

TREASURE #3: POTENTIAL

Mountain climbing has become increasingly popular in recent years. Increasing numbers of people from all walks of life are tackling the great peaks of the world, including many more women and senior citizens. Even a surprising number of disabled people are climbing, such as Tom Whittaker, who lost his right foot to a car accident in 1979. On May 27, 1998, he astounded the world by becoming the first amputee to stand on the summit of Mt. Everest.

When asked why they climb, many of these people give the same answer: "I want to find out what I'm made of."

Indeed, there's nothing like a great mountain to show you what you're made of. And if that's true of Everest, K2 or Denali, it's even truer of the mountain of the Lord. Every step up the mountain of the Lord will demand something of you. Every aspect of your character will be put to the test at various stages. Of course, there will be great victories and moments of euphoria, but there also will be many hardships and unexpected challenges that will test your endurance, your self-discipline and, ultimately, your faith.

This undoubtedly is why so many people start climbing

the mountain of the Lord, but don't stick with it. They see the heart-stopping beauty of the mountain in the distance and hear uplifting stories of how other climbers have been blessed, so they gather their gear and join an expedition. But in no time, they're retracing their steps, chucking their gear as they go. They simply had no idea it was going to be so hard.

I know that if there were stairs—or better yet, an elevator—built into the side of Mt. Everest, a lot more people would be standing on her summit. But it would be a hollow conquest, for only those accomplishments that cost us something have value. Any climb that fails to stretch you is a waste of time.

Be advised as you approach the mountain of the Lord that you will be stretched if you choose to climb, probably in ways you never dreamed. But in the stretching, as painful as it may be at times, will come the realization of your potential, which, for a lot of people, is long overdue. Maybe you're a person who has been a valley dweller for too many years, always knowing in your heart that you could (and should) push yourself and reach for something more. If so, then let this book be your challenge to get up and get with it. I like what George Eliot said: "It's never too late to become what you might have been."

TREASURE #4: PEACE

The fact that you're still reading this book tells me one of two things. Either you're my mother, or you're very interested in climbing the mountain of the Lord. If the latter is the case, there's a simple truth you need to face. Once the notion of climbing has settled in your heart, you'll never find peace until you go for it.

In the early 1990s, Poinciana Christian Church had a small sign by the side of the road about eight miles north of our building location. The sign wasn't fancy by any means. It sported no flashing lights, bright colors or clever sayings. It simply informed motorists that PCC was eight miles straight ahead.

At times, I wondered if the sign did us any good at all. Nobody ever mentioned it, and as the area around it kept growing and changing, it seemed to become less and less conspicuous. If it had been costing us anything significant in terms of money or manpower for upkeep, I probably would have been in favor of taking it down. But that would have been a mistake. Little did I know that the Lord was using that sign in a mighty way.

Every day a young woman in her mid-twenties drove past that sign on her way home from work. She was extremely intelligent, a graduate of the University of Florida, and had an excellent job in research and development for a large company. She made good money, lived in a beautiful home, was married to a handsome, talented guy and drove a new red sports car. By the world's standards, she had everything. But she wasn't happy. Behind the pasted-on smiles were some deep, unresolved issues from her childhood and a rapidly deteriorating marriage.

Every day when she drove past that sign, her eyes seemed to be drawn to it. She never heard an audible voice, yet the Lord seemed to say to her, "You'll never be happy until you get right with Me." As the days and weeks passed, the sign began to haunt her, and at times she even steeled herself to look the other way when she drove by.

Finally, when she couldn't stand it anymore, she came to our church. She walked in, found a seat in the back row next to the exit, sat through the service and sprinted for the parking lot as soon as the last amen was uttered. As she got into her car, she said aloud, "There, God, I did it. I went to church. Now are you satisfied?"

He wasn't.

For the next three months, she stayed away from church, but drove by the sign every day. It sparked nagging memories of the worship service she had attended. She'd expected it to be dull, but it wasn't. She'd planned to put it out of her mind as soon as she walked out the door, but she couldn't. And with every day that passed, the thought of going back—this time for keeps—grew stronger and stronger. Finally, she gave in and returned.

That was over thirteen years ago. Today she and her husband (yes, the same one) are happy climbers, having found on the mountain of the Lord all the treasures they never were going to find in the valley in which they'd been living.

When I think about their story, I'm reminded again of what an amazing God we serve—a God who can use a simple road sign to turn somebody's life upside down. But even more than that, He is a God who loves so deeply that He relentlessly woos and pursues the lost. Understand this, my friend: If the notion to climb has settled in your heart, you might as well go for it. It's the only way you're ever going to find peace.

✳   ✳   ✳

As we conclude this first leg of our journey, I hope your chin is tilted upward and that you are seeing the mountain of the Lord in a whole new light. I hope you can see that it's more than just an escape route from the problems of life. I hope you can see that it offers unspeakable treasures to those who commit themselves to its slopes. And I hope, above all, that you can hear the Lord telling you—perhaps through something as simple as a road sign—that it's time to climb!

Two

GIRD UP YOUR MIND

*"There are two kinds of climbers . . .
smart ones and dead ones."*

—Don Whillans

If asked to name a dangerous sport, most people would quickly mention football, auto racing or boxing. But those sports are mere child's play compared to mountain climbing.

For example, K2 is the second-tallest mountain in the world, but according to most experts, the hardest to climb. There is approximately one fatality for every four successful summits. By comparison, Mt. Everest is a cakewalk. Over the years, it has produced one fatality for every ten successful summits.

Because mountain climbing is so dangerous, it's important to be thinking clearly at all times. In such a hostile environment, even one careless act can lead to a sudden, horrifying death. In 1998, Chris Hooyman, an experienced climber and guide on Alaska's Denali (Mt. McKinley), saw a member of his party slip and fall, then struggle to get up. Chris, who had summitted Denali three times, foolishly unhooked his rope and turned to help the man to his feet. In the blink of an eye, he slipped and fell to his death, leaving his companions staring in horror.

As we stand at the foot of the Lord's mountain, we must realize that it, too, is a dangerous place. Some might assume that because it's the Lord's mountain, climbing will be easy and dangers will be few. But just the opposite is true. The Bible makes it clear that wherever Christians are striving for God, Satan will be lurking. First Peter 5:8 says it best: "Be careful! Watch out for attacks from the Devil, your great enemy. He prowls around like a roaring lion, looking for some victim to devour." Can't you picture a hungry mountain lion, peering out from behind a boulder, watching for an unsuspecting climber, just waiting for the right moment to pounce?

But you don't have to be a victim! By thinking clearly and constantly, you can protect yourself from harm.

THINK CLEARLY

Several years ago, one of the world's largest producers of ketchup and barbecue sauces decided to package a new line of barbecue sauce in a spray bottle. The idea was to make the grilling experience easier and cleaner. No more sloppy basting brushes. No more splashing barbecue sauce on your clothes or dribbling it on your shoes (as I seem prone to do). And best of all, no more burning your fingers by getting them too close to the fire. Most analysts agreed it was a great idea, but the people in the packaging department doomed it by not using their heads.

They designed a bottle that was way too tall. It was so tall that it could only sit on the top shelf at most supermarkets, putting it out of the sight and reach of most shoppers. It was also too tall to sit upright on most refrigerator shelves, forcing consumers to lay it on its side where it became an annoying space hog. And to top it off, the bottle's shape made it look more like a glass cleaner than a sweet-tasting condiment. Naturally, the product flopped, which was bad news for everybody except the people who make aprons, spot removers and basting brushes.

Often, a little clear thinking is the difference between success and failure. Here are three things about which you *must* think clearly if you're serious about climbing the mountain of the Lord successfully.

First, you must think clearly about the PATH you will follow.

Every mountain offers a route to the top that is safer and more desirable to the average climber than any other. This is not to suggest that every mountain has an easy route to the top, but there will always be one that offers the best chance of success. Finding it is the hard part. On Everest, English and Swiss expeditions probed the mountain for fifty years before Sir Edmund Hillary and Tenzing Norgay finally found a way to the summit.

Thankfully, our Lord has not left us to search for a path to follow. Jesus said, *"I am the way,* the truth, and the life. No one can come to the Father except through me" (John 14:6, author's emphasis). And again, Peter said, "Christ, who suffered for you, is your example. *Follow in his steps"* (1 Peter 2:21, author's emphasis). Such statements eliminate the need for us to spend time looking for a way up the mountain of the Lord. If we simply follow in Jesus' footsteps, we can't go wrong.

Some climbers, however, have not been content to follow in Jesus' footsteps and have wandered off in search of alternate routes, which are less demanding and more enjoyable. Three of the most popular ones are:

> **The Road of Religion.** You'll eventually get to the top if you just go to church on a regular basis and faithfully observe all the rituals of your particular denomination.

> **The Footpath of Feelings.** If you *feel* like you're on the right track, then you must be.

> **The Way of Works.** Just be nice and do good to your fellow man, and you'll eventually get to the top.

When I think about these alternate routes and the many people who have chosen to follow them, I'm reminded of

Proverbs 14:12: "There is a path before each person that seems right, but it ends in death."

When our Lord said, "No one can come to the Father except through me," he couldn't have been any clearer. Jesus is the path.

Second, you must think clearly about the PEOPLE you will follow.

Anyone who's new to the sport of mountain climbing will need quality instruction and an experienced guide when he or she gets out on the slopes. Fortunately, the American Mountain Guides Association (AMGA) has established a system of standards and qualifications to help beginners find a qualified instructor.

Spiritual climbers on the mountain of the Lord need quality instruction and guide service, too, although I'm afraid it isn't always easy to find. There are many religious voices crying, "Follow me! I know where I'm going!" But there is no *Spiritual Mountain Guides Association* to check credentials and offer warnings and recommendations. Extreme caution is needed when choosing someone to follow because the Bible makes it clear that many spiritual climbing instructors who appear qualified really aren't. Remember, Jesus said, "Not all people who sound religious are really godly. They may refer to me as 'Lord,' but they still won't enter the kingdom of heaven" (Matt. 7:21).

Let me suggest three tests you should apply to any potential teacher, mentor or guide.

Test #1: Is he or she following in Jesus' footsteps? It's important to remember that even the greatest leaders should be followers themselves. Look closely at the person and see if his/her lifestyle is what you would expect from a true follower of Jesus. If you regularly witness behaviors or attitudes that seem inconsistent with a Christlike spirit, or if you feel that certain fruits of the Spirit are missing from the person's life, then continue your search.

Test #2: Is he or she an experienced climber? When I step onto an airplane, I always take a peek to the left and try to get a look at the pilot's hair. If it's got a little gray in it, I feel better. Although it may not always be true, gray hair speaks to me of seasoning and experience, which are valuable commodities in the kind of high-pressure situations that flying a plane often produces. Make sure the person who's leading you up the mountain of the Lord has experienced a spiritual rockslide or two and has negotiated a few steep ledges. It would make little sense to follow someone who's as green as you are.

Test #3: Has he/she taught other people to climb well? Jesus said, "The way to identify a tree or a person is by the kind of fruit that is produced" (Matt. 7:20). A skilled mountain guide's "fruit" should consist of more than just books or articles about mountain climbing. He should be "growing" other climbers. In fact, the best teachers in any arena often are surpassed by their students because they don't just impart knowledge, they instill passion. Before you choose a mentor in the faith, look around and see who else is climbing because of his/her influence.

It's important to think clearly when you choose a person to follow because that person will cause you to soar or to stumble. Stumbling is bad enough when you're walking on flat valley ground, but when you're clinging to the side of a mountain hundreds or thousands of feet above the valley, much more is at stake. Even a slight misstep can mean death.

Third, you must think clearly about the PROCEDURES you will follow.

Mountain climbing is like flying an airplane in a couple of respects. Not only do you achieve altitude in the process, but there are certain safety procedures you must follow if you hope to survive. No pilot takes off without running a thorough check to make sure all of the plane's systems are working properly, and no mountain climber leaves base camp without checking his gear. Just imagine the horror of hanging from the side of a two-hundred-foot cliff and suddenly noticing that your rope is badly frayed! No wonder the Bible says, "Don't lose sight of good planning" (Prov. 3:21a).

I'm sure it comes as no surprise that there are standard safety procedures for spiritual climbers as well. Here are ten that the Bible stresses:

Keep good company. (1 Cor. 15:33)

Stay sober. (Eph. 5:16)

Listen to people who are older and wiser. (Prov. 1:8–9)

Forgive those who hurt you. (Eph. 4:32)

Be content. (1 Tim. 6:6–10)

Use your gifts. (Rom. 12:6–8)

Focus on the positive. (Phil. 4:8)

Control your tongue. (James 3:2)

Work hard. (2 Tim. 2:15)

Pray without ceasing. (1 Thess. 5:17)

Although these exhortations may seem oppressive at times, they are safety procedures in the truest sense. They are given to keep us from stumbling and falling. To take them lightly is to needlessly flirt with danger. I can tell you that every one of the fallen climbers I have known failed in one or more of these ten areas.

THINK CONSTANTLY

Clear thinking is only helpful if it is done constantly. The nature of life is that even a momentary lapse in judgment can negate a lifetime of good choices. In climbing, you might think that most mental mistakes would be made by beginners, and plenty are. But a surprising number of veteran climbers have suffered and died because of momentary lapses in judgment. For example, in Yellowstone National Park, a guide with extensive backcountry experience went solo hiking with headphones on, listening to music. The guide, who often warned tourists to watch and listen for grizzly bears, somehow forgot his own advice. With music pounding in his ears, he stumbled upon a mother bear and her cubs and was badly mauled.

Veteran climbers on the mountain of the Lord have suffered momentary lapses in judgment as well. Abraham, David and Peter are three cases in point. A closer look at their experiences will reveal the reasons for their mental lapses and serve as vital warnings to us.

Abraham's mental lapses happened because of a WORRY.

On two occasions (Gen. 12:10–20; 20:1–18), Abraham became worried that pagan authorities would kill him and steal his beautiful wife, Sarah. Even though God had promised to protect him and to punish anyone who would dare raise a hand against him (Gen. 12:3), Abraham still worried himself into such a state of anxiety that he started making terrible decisions. Specifically, he ordered Sarah to lie about their relationship and say that she was his sister.

Worry that is unchecked leads to panic, and panic leads to mental lapses. Recently, a man in Texas became worried that his wife was having an affair with a coworker. She denied it, but he didn't believe her and foolishly decided to take matters into his own hands. He went to her office at closing time and waited for the man to come out of the building. When he did, the jealous husband jumped out of his car and attacked him. In the end, the husband was arrested and was further humiliated to discover that he beat up the wrong man. The person he attacked was merely a salesman making a call on the company . . . a man who had never even met his attacker's wife!

Is there a worry that is nagging you as you read this?
Is your marriage growing cold and stale?
Are your finances in shambles?
Are your kids heading in the wrong direction?
Has your health started to deteriorate?

If so, you need to be proactive in dealing with the problem. Unbridled worry produces panic, and panicky people often step outside the realm of good judgment. Get help if you need it, but above all, go back and revisit the promises of Scripture. Let them remind you that God is bigger than any problem you may face. Let His Word develop in you the kind of calm assurance the psalm writer demonstrated when he said, "God is our refuge and strength, always ready to help in times of trouble. So we will not fear, even if earthquakes come and the mountains crumble into the sea" (Ps. 46:1–2).

David's mental lapses happened because of a WALL.

Any student of the life of David will notice that he erected a wall between his public life and his private life. As a soldier and leader of God's people, he consistently sought the Lord's counsel and won victory after victory. But as a family man, he did not consult God and made one foolish mistake after another. For example, he married the daughter of his archenemy, Saul (1 Sam. 18:22–27), he ignored God's law against polygamy (Deut. 17:17; 2 Sam. 5:13), and he stole another man's wife (2 Sam. 11).

It's impossible to read David's story without scratching your head and wondering how such a brilliant man could make such foolish mistakes. But that's what happens when you build a wall around one area of your life and keep God out of it. You're going to lack His wisdom in that area and become very susceptible to foolish mistakes.

Have you compartmentalized your life? Maybe you've erected a wall to keep God out of your business affairs. Or maybe the wall is designed to hide an illicit relationship or a nasty habit, while you publicly go about the business of being a Christian. Ask yourself if there's an area of your life where you repeatedly have made bad choices over the years. I've heard people say, "I'm just unlucky in love" or "I'm unlucky in business." Maybe your problem isn't that you're unlucky, but that you haven't given God access to that area of your life. Tear down the wall that's keeping Him out and your "luck" will begin to change.

Peter's mental lapses happened because of a WEAKNESS.

Peter had several strengths, but one glaring weakness repeatedly got him into trouble: He was impulsive. As I read the Gospels, I cringe when I see him daring to rebuke the Lord (Matt. 16:22), making grandiose promises (Luke 22:33), or pulling out his sword and slicing off Malchus's ear

(John 18:10–11). Even a moment's pause to consider his actions might have spared Peter a world of heartache and embarrassment. But pausing to think was not his strong suit.

Do you have a weakness that causes you to make foolish choices? Maybe, like Peter, you're impulsive. Or maybe you have a hot temper, a lazy streak or an unnatural interest in sensual things. It doesn't matter how intelligent you are, if you don't get busy and bring that weakness under control, it will have you acting like a fool sooner or later. You may even need counseling if the weakness has you in a vice grip. If so, get it. Go through whatever process is necessary to break the hold it has on you. *Anything* that keeps you from thinking clearly at all times simply has to go.

$$* \quad * \quad *$$

One of my favorite movies is *The Wizard of Oz.* I love all the characters, but mostly I'm partial to the Scarecrow. He's so optimistic and full of energy, a wonderful encourager. But because he's made of straw, there's no thinking apparatus in his head. For me, one of the highlights of the film is when he croons his melancholy little song about all the things he'd do if he only had a brain.

Well, you *do* have one! And when you commit yourself to using it . . . to eliminating the worries, walls and weaknesses that cause you to have mental lapses, you will have taken one more step in your preparation for climbing the mountain of the Lord.

JOIN UP WITH AN EXPEDITION

"Two people can accomplish more than twice as much as one; they get a better return for their labor. If one person falls, the other can reach out and help. But people who are alone when they fall are in real trouble."

—King Solomon (Eccl. 4:9–10)

As I write this chapter, there is a stunning news item making headlines all across the country. About a week ago, a twenty-seven-year-old climber named Aron Ralston went on what he thought would be a one-day outing in Blue John Canyon in southeastern Utah. Everything was fine until he reached into a crack in the canyon wall searching for a handhold. As he did, an enormous boulder shifted slightly and pinned his arm. He spent hours trying to free himself, even using ropes and anchors in an effort to create leverage. But with the boulder weighing almost a thousand pounds, he was unsuccessful and eventually realized he was trapped like an animal.

Aron knew he would be missed eventually, so he sat tight, hoping that a search-and-rescue team would arrive before he ran out of food and water. It didn't happen. One day turned into two, two turned into three, and three turned into four. Because he'd only planned to be gone for a day, his food and water supplies disappeared quickly. Finally, on the sixth day, realizing he was going to die if he didn't take bold action, Aron did the unthinkable. He pulled out his pocketknife and began cutting off his arm just below the elbow.

When his arm was severed, he quickly applied a tourniquet and administered what first aid he could. Then, in a mind-boggling demonstration of physical strength, Aron rappelled sixty feet to the ground and began walking to his car, which was parked a couple of miles away. Before he reached his vehicle, he was spotted by a search-and-rescue team that had been combing the area in a helicopter. They picked him up and took him straight to a nearby hospital, where he is as I write these words. It's being reported that he walked into the hospital under his own power, is expected to recover and is already talking about resuming his climbing career.

I think there are two lessons to be learned from Aron's experience.

First, a mountain is no respecter of persons. Aron Ralston is a climber of great skill and even greater experience. He has climbed all forty-nine of Colorado's fourteen-thousand-foot peaks and scaled an incalculable number of canyon walls. His friends have described his climbing exploits as awe-inspiring. But that boulder didn't give a rip. It's been said that when a mountain is hungry, it isn't choosy about who it eats.

Second, Aron's terrifying experience is a reminder that it's risky to climb alone. If something goes wrong, as it can in the blink of an eye, you have no backup. If Aron had taken a friend along, that person could have gone for help, and the outcome likely would have been very different.

Climbing alone on the mountain of the Lord is risky, too. As I said in the last chapter, just because it's the Lord's mountain doesn't mean it's a safe place. Wherever you find people striving for God, you will find Satan lurking. He'll start a rockslide here or an avalanche there, anything to try to cause God's people to lose their grip on faith and go tumbling back toward the valley.

Let me just be blunt at this point.

If you're really serious about climbing the mountain of the Lord, you need to hook up with an expedition. That is, you need to hook up with a church. A church is nothing more than a group of spiritual climbers who have banded together and set their sights on higher ground. They're working together and watching each others' backs. Oh yes, I know there are lots of people who say they can climb better alone. And yes, I'm well aware that you can worship God on a golf course or sitting in a boat at your favorite fishing hole. For almost thirty years, I've heard every conceivable excuse ... every conceivable line of reasoning from the "I-hate-organized-religion" crowd.

I don't care.

I still say you need to hook up with a church.

My reasons are summed up quite nicely in this little verse by Rudyard Kipling:

> Now this is the Law of the Jungle
> As old and as true as the sky;
> And the wolf that shall keep it may prosper,
> But the wolf that shall break it must die.
> As the creeper that girdles the tree trunk,
> The Law runneth forward and back
> For the strength of the pack is the wolf
> And the strength of the wolf is the pack.

As the wolf finds strength in the pack, so the Christian finds strength in the church. Hebrews 10:24–25 says, "Think of ways to encourage one another to outbursts of love and good deeds. And let us not neglect our meeting together, as some people do, but encourage and warn each other, especially now that the day of his coming back is drawing near."

The Bible makes it clear that God wants us to climb together. All I have to do is think back over my years in the ministry to understand why. I can't name even one solo climber I have known who survived long term on the mountain of the

Lord. I've known quite a few who thought they could ... quite a few who broke away from their churches out of anger or frustration and took off on their own. But none of them survived very long. Either they joined up with another church or they gave up climbing altogether and retreated to the valley. Remember, at the very beginning of time, God said that it wasn't good for a man to be alone. It's worth noting that the very first thing He did for Adam was to give him a climbing partner (Gen. 2:18).

If you're not currently part of a church, you need to be looking for one to join. Of course, finding the right one isn't the easiest thing in the world to do. There are lots of churches out there, but many are not desirable. Some have been known to hinder climbers more than they help them. Therefore, you need to be very careful. Before you join any church, there is one key question you should ask:

Are the people camping or climbing?

Let me explain.

One of the first priorities for every Himalayan expedition is to establish Base Camp, which is exactly what the name implies: a *camp* that serves as a *base* of operations. Base Camp will be a cluster of tents set up on the lower slopes of the mountain, just at the point where climbing becomes serious business. Although other smaller camps will be established as the expedition pushes upward, Base Camp is the main headquarters. It will be a supply station, communication center, mess hall, barracks and hospital.

It would be unthinkable for an expedition to go to all the trouble and expense of establishing a Base Camp, and then never climb the mountain, but that is exactly what a lot of churches have done. They have purchased property, built buildings and settled into comfortable routines. They have divided up the chores and developed a system for keeping the camp organized. They have even hired a professional camp superintendent (pastor) to remind people of the rules and encourage full participation in camp activities.

But through it all, they have forgotten to climb!

Before you commit to any church, you need to determine if the people are climbers or campers. Following are five essential characteristics of a climbing church.

CHARACTERISTIC #1: A CLIMBING CHURCH WILL WORSHIP ENTHUSIASTICALLY

All churches hold services at a set time on the weekend, but that doesn't mean they *worship*, and it certainly doesn't mean they worship enthusiastically. I was a guest speaker at a small church years ago. I'd never been there before, knew nothing about the congregation's personality or history, and had never met the preacher. When I walked in about a half-hour before the service, the preacher greeted me and immediately began to apologize for what I was about to observe. He warned me that the people wouldn't sing much, wouldn't show much enthusiasm and probably wouldn't be very friendly. And then he added a curious comment: "But they really do love the Lord."

It's not my place to judge the hearts of those people. Certainly, their preacher knew them better than I did. But I must confess that I found it all very puzzling. The place had all the energy of a morgue at midnight, yet I was being told that the people really loved the Lord. It just didn't add up.

Scripture, as well as everything in my personal experience, tells me that where God is truly loved there will be enthusiasm in worship. Psalm 47:1 says, "Come, everyone, and clap your hands for joy! Shout to God with joyful praise! For the Lord Most High is awesome." Notice the terminology, "the Lord Most *High*." That word "high" seems significant considering our climbing theme, don't you think? It's reminding us that God is above us, that He's higher, greater, more wonderful than anyone or anything we can know in this life. That He, the Most *High* God, has opened a way for us to approach Him is so utterly fantastic that anyone with a heart for climbing simply has to be ecstatic!

Simply put, I would be leery of joining up with any expedition where there seemed to be little enthusiasm for worship because, when all is said and done, worship is climbing. And if the people aren't into climbing, then they must be into camping.

CHARACTERISTIC #2: A CLIMBING CHURCH WILL HAVE A VISION

A vision is nothing more than a specific plan for future growth. Often, it's born in the hearts of a few leaders (because most people are not visionaries) and then thoughtfully and prayerfully shaped according to the congregation's personality and demographic profile. It then will be communicated to the people in a positive fashion and used to shape programs and ministries. A vision may have short-term and long-term components, but it always will make a firm statement: "We're here to climb, not camp."

It's my conviction that every member of a church ought to understand and be able to talk about his church's vision. One obvious reason is that he can't possibly contribute to the success of it if he doesn't understand it. But an equally important reason is that he can't explain it to others if he doesn't understand it himself. I am noticing that, more than ever before, seekers—those who are looking for a church home—are asking a lot of questions about the church's direction and goals. No longer do they just assume that we church leaders know what we're doing. And why should they? There are enough dead and strife-torn churches around that they have every right to be suspicious. As one young man said to me recently, "If I get on this bus, where can I expect to wind up?"

Before you sign on with any expedition, you have a right

to know where you might wind up. You have a right to know *what* mountain you're going to be climbing, *who's* going to be in charge and *how* the summit is going to be approached. If these basic questions produce a lot of stammering and stuttering, you probably ought to look for another expedition.

CHARACTERISTIC #3: A CLIMBING CHURCH WILL BE EVANGELISTIC

Jesus said that he came to seek and save the lost (Luke 19:10) and constantly impressed the importance of evangelism on his followers. He called them to be "fishers of men" (Matt. 4:19) and to go into the whole world making disciples (Matt. 28:18–20). Even as he ascended into heaven he gave a final call to carry the gospel "to the ends of the Earth" (Acts 1:8). Therefore, any church that isn't making an effort to save souls is hardly a *Christian* church, let alone a *climbing* church.

But having said that, let me be quick to offer a word of caution.

Be careful not to judge a church's evangelistic fervor merely by statistics. For example, lots of churches publish their "additions to date" on the front page of their weekly newsletter. Some call it a "circle of evangelism." It will be a little circle (or a big one if the church is having a good year) with a number inside, indicating the number of new members the church has gained during the current calendar year. But does that number tell the whole story?

How many of those new members merely were switching churches?

How many of them disappeared after a few weeks or months?

How many of them were won to the church rather than the Lord?

How many of them were won to the *preacher* rather than the Lord?

I can name several congregations that boast a hundred or more additions per year, but their weekly attendance hasn't changed in years. How can that be? Obviously, there's a hole in the bucket. People are "leaking" out the back door as fast as they're coming in the front door!

The best way to evaluate a church's effectiveness in evangelism is to look beyond the raw numbers. I believe *effort* and *changed lives* are the key. If a congregation honestly is trying to win souls, and if the people who are being added genuinely are being changed by the power of the Holy Spirit, then you can feel pretty certain that you've found a climbing church.

CHARACTERISTIC #4: A CLIMBING CHURCH WILL FIND JOY IN SACRIFICE

I love Paul's picture of the Macedonian Christians in 2 Corinthians 8:1–5. He said, "Though they have been going through much trouble and hard times, their wonderful joy and deep poverty have overflowed in rich generosity" (v. 2). That's one of those statements a person needs to reread to make sure he's not hallucinating. The words "trouble," "hard times" and "poverty" just don't seem to belong in the same sentence with words like "joy," "overflowed," "rich" and "generosity." But there they are, all mingled together, and they make a powerful statement: These were people who found joy in sacrifice.

Not many churches nowadays find joy in sacrifice. In fact, there are a lot of churches that haven't made a real sacrifice in years. A preacher friend of mine told me about a board meeting at his church where the elders and deacons voted unanimously to purchase a new fifteen-passenger van at a cost of almost thirty thousand dollars. Ten minutes later, a request was brought forward on behalf of one of the missionaries the congregation supports. They had had a fire at their base of operation and had lost valuable computer equipment, furniture and supplies. After much haggling, the board voted to send them a measly two hundred dollars, which left the checking account balance at just over ten thousand! My friend was heartsick.

Unfortunately, such a "me-first" attitude is common in many churches. We worship in air-conditioned auditoriums with state-of-the-art lights and sound. We sit on the softest pews and walk on the plushest carpet money can buy. We chauffeur our youth and seniors groups around in late-model vehicles. Yet, we allow our missionaries to subsist on leftovers. We send them our secondhand furniture, obsolete computer equipment and hand-me-down clothing, not to mention our unwanted tools so they can fix their fifteen-year-old vehicles.

I've often thought that one of the best ways to evaluate any church is simply to observe the quality of life of the people the church supports. It's not important that they have the best of everything, but it does say something if they have the *worst* of everything. I thank God for those climbing churches that look beyond themselves and find joy in making sacrifices for others.

CHARACTERISTIC #5: A CLIMBING CHURCH WILL BE HARMONIOUS

Stories about church conflicts are legendary. I remember hearing about a small church in the Midwest where two elders had a falling out over a business deal. For two years, they didn't look each other in the eye or speak to each other. They would sit at the same table during meetings, but never acknowledge each other's existence. They even served together at the communion table, praying over the Lord's Supper and the offering without ever making eye contact. (Personally, I don't know who ought to be more ashamed, the two men who hated each other or the other elders who allowed them to continue serving while behaving in such a sinful manner!)

For the record, God doesn't take kindly to this kind of behavior. Proverbs 6 says that there are several things the Lord hates, and one of them is "a person who sows discord among his brothers" (v. 19). Jesus also indicated that discord is a prescription for disaster. He said, "Any kingdom at war with itself is doomed" (Luke 11:17).

As you look for an expedition to join, keep this in mind: People who are busy climbing have neither the time nor the inclination to quarrel. If a man's eyes are on the summit and his mind is focused on what he has to do to achieve greater elevation in his Christian life, he's not going to be fretting over the foibles of his fellow climbers. So when you encounter Christian people who are fussing and fighting, you can rest assured they are campers, not climbers.

✳   ✳   ✳

As I close this chapter, let me just say that there's no such thing as a perfect expedition. Even the churches that possess all the qualities I've just discussed have plenty of room for improvement. For example, Bob Russell is the preaching minister of the dynamic, seventeen-thousand-member Southeast Christian Church in Louisville, Kentucky. That congregation started with fifty people in 1962, and now is one of the largest and fastest-growing churches in America. Its annual budget has increased from eighteen-thousand dollars a year to eighteen million. Thousands of people have come to Christ as a result of the church's efforts, including the popular writer and speaker Liz Curtis Higgs. Surely, Southeast Christian is a climbing church if ever there was one! Yet, here's what Bob Russell has to say in his book, *When God Builds a Church:*

I can list several areas in our church where our staff agrees we are falling short right now: following up and training volunteers; the landscaping around our new building; traffic flow. I can remind myself of all the reasons we aren't measuring up to a standard of excellence in these areas—and many of them are valid and beyond our control—but it's still disappointing. I have to remember that we'll always be striving for perfection. We'll never reach that goal in this life.

Don't go looking for a perfect expedition. You won't find it. But if you're prayerful, patient and keep the right criteria in mind, eventually you will find a group of climbers who will welcome you into their fellowship and be a tremendous encouragement to you as you work your way up the mountain of the Lord.

Four

GATHER UP YOUR GEAR

*"In parachuting, even a jump master
carries a reserve chute. As a climber, your
main chute is your climbing ability;
your backup is your equipment."*

—John Long

Virtually all sports involve equipment, but few sports are as gear-intensive as climbing. As a general rule, the farther you venture into the wilderness, the more gear you will need. Himalayan expeditions, for example, often carry so much equipment that they resemble army encampments. But even if you're just a weekend warrior climbing in the foothills near your home, you will still need to adequately prepare for the elements and the challenges of the rock. Even the best climbers fall, and when they do, their gear is all that stands between them and a severe injury or sudden death.

In this chapter, I want to talk about the *tools* you will need as a climber on the mountain of the Lord and a few *rules* you should keep in mind.

TOOLS

God has been gracious enough to itemize the climber's gear for us in a single passage of Scripture, Ephesians 6:13–18 (NASB):

Therefore, take up the full armor of God, that you may be able to resist in the evil day, and having done everything, to stand firm. Stand firm therefore, having girded your loins with truth, and having put on the breastplate of righteousness, and having shod your feet with the preparation of the gospel of peace; in addition to all, taking up the shield of faith with which you will be able to extinguish all the flaming missiles of the evil one. And take the helmet of salvation, and the sword of the Spirit, which is the word of God. With all prayer and petition pray at all times in the Spirit, and with this in view, be on the alert with all perseverance and petition for all the saints.

We've already established that our enemy is prowling the mountain of the Lord like a lion, looking for climbers to devour, so it's not surprising that Paul's description of the climber's gear takes on a military tone. Although his word pictures seem foreign to us, he wisely used imagery that any first-century reader would have been able to grasp. Roman soldiers were everywhere in those days, intimidating the populace with their scowling faces, spiffy garb and polished weaponry. To compare the Christian's essential gear with a Roman soldier's clearly was a stroke of genius.

Let's look briefly at each of the six pieces of equipment Paul says you'll need if you intend to climb the mountain of the Lord.

First, you'll need the BELT OF TRUTH because climbers must be able to move freely.

Every Roman soldier wore a belt around his waist to keep his loose outer garments from flopping about. There were times in battle when a quick movement could mean the difference between life and death, and the last thing he needed was to be impaired by an unruly tunic.

To picture a Christian's belt as being made of truth is particularly insightful. Jesus said, "You will know the truth, and the truth will *set you free*" (John 8:32, author's emphasis). No climber who is wearing the belt of truth will be impaired by subtle deceptions or false doctrine. He will be *free* to move quickly and confidently, negotiating even the trickiest maneuvers with great agility.

Second, you'll need the BREASTPLATE OF RIGHTEOUSNESS because Satan always aims at a climber's heart.

The Roman soldier wore on his upper body a metal plate that was hammered into the shape of a human torso. It covered his heart and vital organs, which were understood to be the parts of the body that were most in need of protection. Even today, police officers in the line of duty often leave their arms, legs, hands, feet and faces exposed, but wear body armor to cover their hearts.

Satan always takes dead aim at the climber's heart. He doesn't care how gifted you are. He doesn't care how much potential you have. He knows that if he can just cause you to lose heart, you're finished. And sure enough, there are millions of valley dwellers who used to be climbers, but at some point a well-aimed arrow broke their hearts and caused them to give up. That's why Solomon said, "Above all else, guard your heart, for it affects everything you do" (Prov. 4:23).

Righteousness is a perfect shield for the heart because it protects against the single most common cause of discouragement in Christians: guilt. Picture Judas's disemboweled body hanging from a tree, and you'll begin to understand the power of Satan to contaminate the heart of a climber, to fill him with guilt and to cause him to give up.

Third, you'll need the SHOES OF THE GOSPEL because every climber needs sure footing.

Most Roman soldiers were infantrymen, which means their lives often depended on their feet. A soldier with ill-fitting shoes or blisters on his feet would have moved slowly and awkwardly and would have been an easier target for the enemy. Though a far cry from the Nikes and Reeboks to which modern man has become accustomed, a Roman soldier's shoes still were the very best money could buy.

Sure footing on the mountain of the Lord is accomplished by always stepping within the boundaries set by the Gospel. Some ledges and cracks look inviting, but actually can be very dangerous. Many a climber has stepped on a seemingly solid jut of rock, only to have it give way and send him reeling. Thankfully, God thought of a simple way to direct our steps and keep us from falling. He gave us the Gospel, the written record of a perfect life. 1 Peter 2:21 says, "Christ, who suffered for you, is your example. *Follow in his steps*" (author's emphasis).

Fourth, you'll need the SHIELD OF FAITH because climbers often encounter projectiles.

The Roman soldier's personal shield was not the large, head-to-toe variety. That would have been much too heavy and would have restricted his movement and agility. Instead, his shield was small and round, perhaps the size of a modern trash-can lid. It was strapped to the soldier's forearm and designed to be whipped about quickly in order to deflect swinging swords, fiery arrows or thrusting spears.

As climbers on the mountain of the Lord, we also need to be able to deflect projectiles. In New Testament times, stones were hurled at God's people (Acts 7:58–60). Now we're more apt to have gossip, criticism, ridicule and false accusations thrown our way. Although the approach may be slightly more civilized, the enemy's goal is the same: knock as many climbers as possible off the mountain.

When projectiles are flying, faith is the shield that can save our lives. In describing climbers of old, the Bible says, "Some were mocked, and their backs were cut open with whips. Others were chained in dungeons. Some died by stoning, and some were sawed in half; others were killed with the sword. Some went about in skins of sheep and goats, hungry and oppressed and mistreated" (Heb. 11:36–37). That's some serious artillery! Yet, the chapter makes it clear that it was their faith that kept them going. As deadly as they were, the projectiles failed to knock those true believers off the mountain.

Fifth, you'll need the HELMET OF SALVATION because a climber's mind must be clear at all times.

The Roman soldier's helmet was made of metal and helped protect him from being disoriented by a blow to the head. In battle, even a moment of fuzzy thinking could give the enemy an advantage and cost the soldier his life.

Climbers wear helmets because one of the greatest dangers they face is from falling rock. All it takes is one chunk of granite landing squarely on your noggin to leave you impaired for the rest of your life. Salvation is the perfect headgear for climbers on the mountain of the Lord because it is the ultimate gift of God, the most precious possession of every climber. Keeping your mind wrapped in thoughts of your salvation will prevent negative thinking and, ultimately, negative behavior. Paul said that the secret to staying on track in the Christian life is to stay focused on the ultimate prize (Phil. 3:13–14).

Sixth, you'll need the SWORD OF THE SPIRIT because sometimes a climber's best defense is a good offense.

The Roman soldier's sword was sheathed to his belt and ready to be drawn in an instant. Primarily, it was an offensive weapon used in hand-to-hand combat, and it truly was a thing to be feared. The swing of a Roman sword could sever a hand, an arm or even a head. You may recall that the high priest's servant, Malchus, lost his right ear to a sword impulsively swung by Peter (John 18:10). Had Peter's aim been a little better, Malchus probably would have lost much more than his ear!

Paul clearly says that the Christian's sword is the word of God. And what a marvelous sword it is! Hebrews 4:12 says that the word of God is "sharper than the sharpest knife." It is the one piece of equipment that strikes fear in the heart of the climber's ultimate enemy, the prowling mountain lion, because it is the one weapon for which he has no defense. He has schemes to twist truth, pervert righteousness and undermine faith, but he stands as helpless as a kitten when confronted with the Word of God. Read again the temptations of Christ (Matt. 4:1–11) and relish the impotence of Satan as he stood against a few well-chosen Scripture quotations. The good news is that any climber can render Satan equally as impotent by swinging this awesome weapon.

RULES

Now that we've inventoried our gear, let me offer some important rules to keep in mind.

Rule #1: Don't be deceived by people who appear to be climbing without gear.

In the movie *Cliffhanger*, there is an exciting scene where Sylvester Stallone is in a desperate race against time. The camera shows a close-up of his grimacing face as he works his way up the face of a steep cliff. As the camera pulls back, we begin to see that he is climbing in a T-shirt (with muscles rippling, of course), although the temperature is sub-freezing. We also notice that he's climbing without any gear. Without gear? Then surely it must not be much of a cliff. Ah, but it is! The camera continues to pull back, and we see that our boy is merely a tiny speck, climbing straight up a huge rock wall that appears to be hundreds, if not thousands of feet high.

Only in Hollywood, my friend. It simply wouldn't happen in real life. As one climber so eloquently put it: "There's another name for what he's doing: suicide!"

There are a lot of people who claim to be climbing the mountain of the Lord without gear. You've probably met people who boast about their relationship with God, even though they give no evidence of wearing any of the armor of God. They don't walk in the truth. They aren't committed to righteousness. They aren't into the Bible. In some cases, they don't even go to church, but they want you to believe that they're reaching great heights on the mountain of the Lord.

Don't believe it.

If you want to climb the mountain of the Lord, you must properly equip yourself. You can get by without gear if all you want to do is *think* about climbing or *talk* about climbing or *criticize* other climbers. But if you actually want to climb, you've got to gear up.

Rule #2: Don't let your gear deteriorate.

Remember that you're going to be depending on your gear to save your neck. Just as a mountaineer would be foolish to start up Everest with a frayed rope or grimy carabiners, so a Christian would be foolish to start up the mountain of the Lord with anything less than a wholehearted commitment to truth, righteousness, faith and the word of God. This is not to suggest that a person must be fully mature in all of these areas before he can start climbing. After all, we grow as we climb.

But there must be an understanding that these are the most critical areas that need constant attention.

I should also say it's the climber's responsibility to maintain his own gear. Over the years, I have met quite a few Christians who have been quick to blame others when their own spiritual lives began to deteriorate. I recall one lady who visited our church recently. She had numerous problems and a very shallow commitment to the Lord. When we sat down to visit, she summed up her difficulties with this statement: "I just wasn't being fed in the church I was attending. The preacher was boring, and I couldn't get anything out of his sermons. It's no wonder I've gotten so far off track." She honestly believed the preacher was to blame for the deterioration of *her* gear.

As tactfully as possible, I tried to suggest that it would take a lot more than a few boring sermons to cause the kind of spiritual decay the woman was experiencing. And sure enough, as the conversation progressed, it became apparent that she had not been committing herself to the basic disciplines of worship, prayer, Bible study and service. She had grown lazy spiritually, pure and simple.

If you're going to climb the mountain of the Lord, understand that you must maintain your equipment. Examine yourself daily to make sure it's not deteriorating.

Rule #3: Don't depend on someone else's gear to save you.

When two climbers are on the side of a mountain, one doesn't say to the other, "Mind if I borrow your rope?" Or, "I forgot my ice axe. Do you have one you're not using?" Every climber takes inventory and makes sure he has everything he needs before he takes a single step toward the mountain.

Oddly, some climbers on the mountain of the Lord seem to think they don't need every piece of equipment as long as their climbing companions are fully equipped. For example, I've had people tell me, "I don't study the Bible much. I figure if I ever have a question I can just ask you." That makes about as much sense as a soldier marching into the teeth of battle without a weapon, telling himself that he'll just borrow one from a friend if things get dicey. Doesn't it stand to reason that an ill-equipped person would be the enemy's first target?

I encourage you to read Paul's passage about the armor of God again. Notice that verse 11 bluntly says, "Put on *all* of God's armor" (author's emphasis). The last thing you want to do is find yourself in a tight spot and not have all the protection you need.

Rule #4: Don't forget to pray.

Paul closes the Ephesians passage by mentioning prayer. Clearly, he was concerned that a Christian all decked out from head to toe in armor might think he was invincible. Of course, that isn't true. Armor alone never has guaranteed safety for any soldier. If it did, Goliath would have defeated David! Paul's point is that, ultimately, it's the Lord who protects you. Yes, you must do your part and equip yourself for the challenge, but in the end you cannot succeed without God's help.

The Union Internationale des Associations D'Alpinisme (UIAA) is the internationally recognized authority for setting standards for climbing equipment. If you see any piece of climbing equipment that has the UIAA label, you know it has met the strictest safety standards. As I was researching this chapter, I ran across an interesting fact: A rope approved by the UIAA never has snapped in a fall. That's pretty impressive. It tells me I can trust the UIAA.

And when it comes to climbing the mountain of the Lord, I can trust God's equipment ratings because no climber on the mountain of the Lord ever has been overcome by the enemy while decked out in the full armor of God. This equipment works, which means you can climb with confidence!

Are you ready?

Then gather up your gear and let's go. It's time to climb!

Part Two:

THE PROCESS

I'm pressing on the upward way
New heights I'm gaining every day
Still praying as I'm onward bound
Lord, plant my feet on higher ground

Johnson Oatman and Charles H. Gabriel
"I'm Passing On," 1898

Five

CLEAN UP YOUR LIFE

*"Climb if you will, but remember
that courage and strength are naught
without prudence, and that momentary negligence
may destroy the happiness of a lifetime. Do nothing
in haste, look well to each step, and from the
beginning think what may be the end."*

—Edward Whymper

I'm glad that when David posed the question, "Who may climb the mountain of the Lord?" he didn't leave us to wonder or speculate. Instead, in Psalm 24:4 he nailed down a specific threefold answer:

Only those whose hands and hearts are pure
Who do not worship idols
And never tell lies.

I find significance in that word "only." These are not *some* of the people who can climb or a *few* of the people who can climb. These are the *only* people who can climb the mountain of the Lord. That makes these requirements vital.

In this chapter and the next two, we'll consider them one at a time.

David's first assertion is that anyone who wants to reach great heights on the mountain of the Lord must have pure hands and a pure heart. In other words, altitude and impurity don't mix.

In Scripture, Joseph and Samson illustrate the point beautifully. Both are well-known figures, but their reputations are as different as night and day. Joseph is universally recognized as a hero of the faith who reached great heights on the mountain of the Lord, while Samson was a valley dweller, a failure, an embarrassment. A striking difference between these two men was their commitment to purity, which the Bible depicts in very graphic terms. First, refresh your memory regarding Joseph's attempted seduction by Potiphar's wife:

*N*ow Joseph was a very handsome and well-built young
man. And about this time, Potiphar's wife began to desire
him and invited him to sleep with her. But Joseph refused.

"Look," he told her, "my master trusts me with everything in his entire household. No one here has more authority than I do! He has held back nothing from me except you, because you are his wife. How could I ever do such a wicked thing? It would be a great sin against God."

She kept putting pressure on him day after day, but he refused to sleep with her, and he kept out of her way as much as possible. One day, however, no one else was around when he was doing his work inside the house. She came and grabbed him by his shirt, demanding, "Sleep with me!" Joseph tore himself away, but as he did, his shirt came off. She was left holding it as he ran from the house. (Gen. 39:6b–12)

I read about a survey where a cross-section of married men were asked if they would have sex with a beautiful woman other than their wives if they were absolutely sure no one ever would find out. Only about 25 percent could state with certainty that they would not. But we can see that, had he been around to participate in the survey, Joseph would have been part of that righteous minority. He had the perfect opportunity to indulge his wildest fantasy with no witnesses and refused.

On the other hand, consider this telling statement about Samson: "One day Samson went to the Philistine city of Gaza and spent the night with a prostitute" (Judg. 16:1).

Unlike Joseph, Samson was the quintessential playboy who lived for the satisfaction of his most carnal desires. He may well have been the most gifted servant of God in all the

Old Testament, but he couldn't take his eyes (or his hands) off the ladies long enough to think about his calling. Need we look any further for an explanation as to why Joseph achieved such greatness as a servant of God while Samson is viewed as a spiritual buffoon?

It's safe to say that no Christian will ever reach great heights on the mountain of the Lord without a serious commitment to holy living. And those who do reach great heights will only be able to stay there if they maintain that commitment. David is a vivid example of a man who climbed a long way, only to find himself tumbling backward when he initiated a sexual relationship with the gorgeous young woman who lived next door.

The question is, how can we make a serious stab at purity when we are stuck in a culture that doesn't even know the meaning of the word? As we begin the new millennium, sex is everywhere. Pornographic materials show up in your e-mail whether you want them or not. Television commercials use sex to sell everything from beer to disposable razors. Scantily clad teenage pop stars bump and grind like exotic dancers. Even family motel chains offer adult movies with "discreet" payment options, making it easy for those who are weak in this area to cover their tracks. As an elderly friend of mine said recently, "When I was young, you had to go looking for sex. Now it comes looking for you." How true. Satan is more aggressive than ever before, and with so many new technologies at his disposal, why shouldn't he be? He can chip away at our resolve in a myriad of ways.

Let me offer two suggestions that I believe will help you in your pursuit of purity.

ADOPT THE PROPER MIND-SET

America is currently involved in a war on terror. It started with the 9/11 terrorist attacks and has continued throughout the world as we have pursued the killers as well as the organizations and governments that support them. It's a different kind of war, as we now understand. Whereas the movements of yesterday's enemies could be carefully monitored, we now realize that our deadliest enemies can hide right under our noses and strike at our most cherished institutions without a moment's notice.

My friend, you need to understand that you are engaged in a personal war with the ultimate terrorist, Satan. He is shrewd and subtle, has many agents doing his bidding, and his goal is no less than your complete annihilation. Paul said, "For we are not fighting against people made of flesh and blood, but against the evil rulers and authorities of the unseen world, against those mighty powers of darkness who rule this world, and against wicked spirits in the heavenly realms" (Eph. 6:12).

When I counsel people who are struggling in the area of personal holiness, I often find that they don't take Satan seriously enough. They see him more as a trickster than an enemy. Recently, I spoke to a young husband whose bad habits were threatening his marriage and his job. When I brought up the subject of Satan's influence on his life, he simply shrugged and said, "I know he's always trying to trip me up." My response was, "No, he's not trying to trip you up. He's trying to *destroy* you."

Do you understand this? Have you grasped the fact that Satan's purpose is not to embarrass you, but to crush you? Do you realize that those little temptations he puts in your path are not just stumbling blocks, but land mines? Their purpose is not to make you fall down and go boom, but to blow your leg off! Remember, Jesus referred to Satan as a murderer (John 8:44).

I mentioned Samson earlier. Go back and read about his encounter with Delilah in Judges 16. He underestimated her. He thought her attempts to learn the secret of his strength were just a childish game, so he played along. He was a good sport. He humored her. And when all was said and done, his strength was gone, his eyeballs were sitting in the Philistines' trophy case, and he was bound in chains.

Some game.

If you want to make progress toward purity, you must adopt the proper mind-set.

ADVANCE IN THE PROPER MANNER

It's important to have the right mindset when pursuing purity, but it's equally important to have a sensible plan of attack. Here are four strategies that I believe will help you make solid progress in the direction of personal holiness.

Strategy #1: Be ready.

In the spring of 2001, the world lost one of its most amazing mountaineers. Babu Chiri Sherpa was universally recognized as the champion of all Himalayan climbers. He had climbed Mt. Everest ten times, including an unbelievable seventeen-hour sprint from Base Camp to summit without the use of bottled oxygen. He was also the only person to have spent a night on top of Mt. Everest, which he also accomplished without bottled oxygen. But on April 29, he fell one hundred feet down a crevasse to his death. Friends said he was walking around Camp II taking pictures and simply wasn't watching his step.

How strange it is that a man who brought the tallest mountain in the world to its knees couldn't survive a casual stroll around the outskirts of his camp. What a striking reminder that bad things can happen in places that appear safe. That's why Paul said, "If you think you are standing strong, be careful, for you, too, may fall into the same sin" (1 Cor. 10:12).

You must never get the idea that you are out of the devil's reach. Even if you do your best to avoid worldly people and environments, you can still run into temptation. For example, studies show that a majority of Christian people who indulge in extramarital affairs do so with people they meet at church—*not* at the local singles bar or in a spicy Internet chat room, but at a Sunday school class party! And it usually starts very innocently.

Eyes meet and linger a little longer than is appropriate.

Smiles are exchanged.

Shoulders brush in passing.

Mildly flirtatious words are spoken.

And it all happens in the context of wholesome fellowship. Often, these exchanges are so subtle they're not even noticed by anyone except the parties involved. Yet, they spark dangerous thought patterns that can lead to sinful behavior faster than you can say, "David and Bathsheba." Don't ever think that because you're in the company of Christian people (or because you're *not* in the company of worldly people), you can afford to relax. Many Christians, although well-intentioned, are spiritually weak and emotionally vulnerable, making them prime targets for Satan.

Be ready at all times!

Strategy #2: Be radical.

Jesus said, "So if your eye—even if it is your good eye—causes you to lust, gouge it out and throw it away. It is better for you to lose one part of your body than for your whole body to be thrown into hell. And if your hand—even if it is your stronger hand—causes you to sin, cut it off and throw it away. It is better for you to lose one part of your body than for your whole body to be thrown into hell" (Matt. 5:29–30).

Obviously, Jesus does not intend for the church to become a legion of half-blind, helpless, wheelchair-bound amputees. He's simply making the point that when it comes to the pursuit of purity, you have to be willing to take radical measures.

Like a young man named Matt.

Matt is a gifted salesman, a handsome guy who dresses well and has a magnetic personality. Women quite naturally are attracted to him. Fortunately, as a happily married Christian man, he's not attracted to them.

Well, not usually.

One day, he met a potential customer whom he found simply captivating. She had the whole package: beauty, brains, a great sense of humor and a smile that would melt the polar ice cap. During their initial discussion, Matt found himself enjoying her company for reasons that had nothing to do with business. He let his eyes drift over her body when her head was turned and found himself making flirtatious comments that were completely out of character for him. To his delight, she responded with several teasing comments of her own and coolly suggested that they continue their "negotiation" over dinner at one of her favorite restaurants. Matt was just about to accept her invitation when his cell phone rang. He unclipped the phone from his belt, looked at the Caller ID and saw that it was his wife. Just seeing her name in the tiny window jolted him. In that instant, Matt came to his senses and saw his behavior in a whole new light. After talking with his wife, he declined the woman's dinner invitation and politely excused himself. The next day, he passed her portfolio on to an associate and determined never to see her again. And yes—in case you're wondering—the woman became one of the company's biggest clients and earned Matt's associate thousands of dollars in commissions.

Naturally, the associate thought Matt was crazy for giving up such a client, but Matt didn't regret it. He said, "Sure, it cost me some money to walk away. But it might have cost me a whole lot more than money had I not walked away." This is the essence of what Jesus was talking about in Matthew 5:29–30. He wasn't telling us to lop off body parts, but to take a radical "no pain, no gain" approach to the pursuit of purity.

Is there a person, place or thing in your life that makes it hard for you to stay on the straight and narrow? If so, maybe it's time to go under the knife. Maybe it's time to end a relationship.

Or look for another job.

Or find a new secretary.

Or close out your online account.

Or cancel a secret subscription.

Or unhook your cable.

The difference between success and failure in the Christian life can—and often does—boil down to a single decision: to be or not to be . . . radical.

Strategy #3: Be reliant.

The thing I've noticed about being radical is that it's easy when you're fired up. A good book, an inspiring sermon, a heart-rending song or a Christian convention are just a few of the things that can make me willing to charge hell with a squirt gun. Unfortunately, there are times when none of those things are available to me. There are times when life demands that I step into a hostile environment and face people and circumstances that stand in opposition to my faith. Those are critical times—times when the enemy licks his chops. But I have no reason to fear as long as I am relying on God's power and not my own.

A great verse of Scripture—but one that is often overlooked—is 2 Timothy 2:1. In that verse, Paul says to Timothy, "Be strong with the special favor God gives you in Christ Jesus." When I read that verse, my eyes immediately are drawn to those two words, "special favor." Special favors are always good, aren't they?

When my wife gives me a backrub, that's a special favor.

When my friends throw me a surprise birthday party, that's a special favor.

When a staff member buys my lunch, that's a *really* special favor!

I admit it...I *love* special favors!

So what is the special favor from God to which Paul is referring? I believe it's simply the strength we need to endure and overcome the challenges of life. Timothy was in a difficult ministry and was being tempted on a variety of fronts. From Paul's letter, we can surmise that he was being tempted to water down his preaching (2 Tim. 4:2–5), to run from suffering (2:3), to indulge his carnal desires (2:22) and to indulge in foolish arguments with combative church members (2:23). But Paul exhorted him to find his strength in God's special favor. It's the same special favor Paul was thinking of when he said, "I can do everything with the help of Christ who gives me the strength I need" (Phil. 4:13). It must also have been in Paul's mind when he said, "I am glad to boast about my weakness, so that the power of Christ may work through me" (2 Cor. 12:9b).

Trust me. What worked for Paul and Timothy will work for you. You, too, can resist even the toughest temptations if you will rely on the special favor of God. I don't care how many times you've given in to that secret sin that drives you crazy with desire one minute and shame the next. I don't care how many times you've sworn you'd never indulge again, only to turn right around the next day and dive in head first. Satan wants you to believe it's hopeless. He wants you to think you've given it your best shot and come up short. But you *haven't* given it your best shot until you quit trying to do it by yourself and start relying on God's strength.

Strategy #4: Be resilient.

Because our culture is so polluted, any person who decides to pursue purity is in for a struggle. It doesn't matter how much you love God or how committed you are to righteous living, there will be days when your humanity will get the best of you and you'll fall flat on your face. Some days you'll be the windshield, and some days you'll be the bug.

Of course, we never should minimize moral failure, but neither should we blow it out of proportion. Just thirty minutes ago, I received a phone call from a friend in the Midwest, telling me that a mutual friend of ours in the ministry has fallen into sin and is losing both his marriage and his job. But that wasn't the worst news. By far the most alarming part of the story is that our friend, in his frustration and shame, apparently has given up the struggle for righteousness. I'm told he has a "what's the use?" attitude and has resigned himself to life as an outcast from God and His people.

Even as I write these words, my heart is breaking. But I've seen it before. Judas was so distraught after betraying Jesus that he took his own life (Acts 1:16–18). And others I have known personally have been swept away by the crashing waves of guilt and shame that always accompany moral failure in Christians.

The thing that makes a scenario like this so heartbreaking is that God's grace is greater than all our sin. Whatever my friend has done (or failed to do), God's grace can handle it. The Bible says, "If we confess our sins to him, he is faithful and just to forgive us and to cleanse us from *every wrong*" (1 John 1:9, author's emphasis). That means there's no reason for him to give up! On the contrary, there's every reason for him to humble himself, repent and bounce back!

And that goes for you, too. If, in your struggle for purity, you've started feeling more like the bug than the windshield, don't lose heart. Instead, stop and analyze the situation.

Do you have a readiness problem?

Do you need to be more radical in your dealings with temptation?

Do you need to rely more on God's strength and less on your own?

Chances are, some adjustments in these areas will help. But whatever you do, don't give up the struggle! I promise, you haven't done anything so terrible that you can't find forgiveness in God's grace and restoration in his love. Let Paul's words in 2 Corinthians 4:8–9 be your inspiration:

We are pressed on every side by troubles, but we are not crushed and broken. We are perplexed, but we don't give up and quit. We are hunted down, but God never abandons us. We get knocked down, but we get up again and keep going (author's emphasis).

Before I close this chapter, I want to offer a word of warning. Satan has a little trick he will play on you if you get serious about the pursuit of purity. It's subtle. It's deadly. And it's brilliant. What is this trick? Simply this: He will encourage you to make purity your god, rather than your goal.

When you make purity your goal, you become a light.

When you make purity your god, you become a legalist.

A legalist makes righteousness the only test of fellowship. He puts law above love. He has a rigid view of how things should be done and rejects anyone who doesn't fall in line and get in step. From a distance, he will give the appearance of being very holy, but the closer you get, the more you realize something isn't quite right. There's no mercy, no grace and no humility. There's never any consideration for mitigating circumstances or opposing points of view. Rather, you'll notice a harsh, Gestapo mentality and a "scorched earth" approach to human relationships. Speaking of legalists in Matthew 23:4, Jesus said, "They crush you with impossible religious demands and never lift a finger to help ease the burden."

Satan loves a legalist. He delights in a person who makes the Christian life burdensome and oppressive. Why? Because he knows such a person will do more harm to the body of Christ than a thousand atheists. He knows such a person will obscure the love of Christ, which is the single greatest threat to his effectiveness. Right now I suspect you could name someone in your own circle of acquaintances who has been driven away from the Lord and his people by cold-hearted, judgmental churchmen.

So I beg you to please be careful as you begin your pursuit of purity. Don't get carried away. Stay humble. Offer compassion to those who fall and patience to those who lag behind. Remember, Paul said that a person without love is of no value whatsoever (1 Cor. 13:3).

Make purity your goal, not your god.

Six

FIRM UP YOUR COMMITMENT

*"If there's anything else you want
to accomplish, go do it. When you're finished
and the only passion you have left is this
mountain, then—and only then—
will you be ready to climb."*

—George Mallory

If there's one thing that all great climbers have in common, it's commitment. Some of the most amazing stories of heroism, survival, perseverance and sheer toughness I've ever heard have come out of the climbing culture.

Take Hugh Herr, for example.

It was 1982 when Hugh and his buddy, Jeff Batzer, went climbing on Mt. Washington in New Hampshire. It was to be a challenging, but enjoyable one-day climb, much like the many others they'd already accomplished. Instead, it turned into a fight for survival as a howling winter storm pinned them down for three days. With no sleeping bag, tent or food, they had no choice but to burrow into the snow for shelter. They hugged each other to keep from freezing to death, but the minus-twenty-degree temperatures still took a terrible toll on their bodies. After a harrowing rescue and an extended hospital stay, both of Hugh's legs had to be amputated at the knee because of a severe case of frostbite.

During his hospital stay, Hugh promised family and friends that he would climb again, legs or no legs—and not just climb again, but climb better. So intense was his commitment to climbing that even before he was released from the rehab hospital, he slipped out with a pair of artificial legs, made his way to the cliffs that jut over the Susquehanna River and pulled his body across the rocky face. Incredibly, just seven months after losing his legs, he was doing two-hundred pull-ups a day and climbing rocks that demanded world-class strength and skill.

Oh yes, and one more thing. At the time, Hugh Herr was a seventeen-year-old high-school student.

Now in his late thirties, he is a graduate of MIT and holds a doctorate in biophysics from Harvard. He recently established the Hugh Herr Institute for Human Rehabilitation in Cambridge, Massachusetts. As of this writing, he holds seven patents on prosthetic devices that are designed to provide increased mobility for the disabled and the elderly. And to top it off, he is an instructor in physical medicine and rehabilitation at both Harvard *and* MIT.

Hugh Herr's stunning accomplishments cannot be explained by his physical ability. The man has no legs. Nor are they explained by his intelligence. There are millions of brilliant people leading wasted lives. No, his greatness is explained by his level of commitment to whatever task he's undertaking. Whether climbing, studying or inventing, he simply will not be distracted or deterred.

People like Hugh Herr remind us that the height of our accomplishments will equal the depth of our convictions. David understood this. That's why he said that those who climb the mountain of the Lord must be people "who do not worship idols" (Ps. 24:4b). In other words, they must be single-minded. They must have no passion that even comes close to the passion they have for God. They must be unshakable in their devotion to him.

As one who has been climbing the mountain of the Lord for many years, I can tell you that commitment is sometimes the only thing that keeps me putting one foot in front of the other. There are days when commitment is the only thing that stands between me and an all-out retreat back to the valley. The same will be true for you. If you're relying on excitement, enthusiasm or enjoyment to keep you going, your days on the mountain are numbered. Those things simply can't sustain you long term. But if you firm up your commitment and determine to let it carry you through the hard times, you'll be fine.

Let me share two wonderful facts about commitment.

COMMITMENT IS THE SECRET TO OUTLASTING OPPONENTS

Yes, there are people who will oppose your climbing efforts. Some of them may even be members of your own expedition. Basically, they'll be divided into two groups.

The Cynics

Years ago, I walked into a conversation late and heard a fellow talking about "yowbutters." I had no idea what he was referring to. Even after listening for a moment, I still wasn't catching on, so I finally spoke up. "What in the world is a yowbutter?" I asked, and he was happy to tell me. "A yowbutter is a person who always says, 'Yeah, but.'" And suddenly the conversation made sense. He was talking about people who have a knack for seeing the dark side of every situation.

You can say, "It's a beautiful day!" and they'll say, "Yeah, but it's supposed to rain tomorrow."

You can say, "The worship music was wonderful at church today!" and they'll say, "Yeah, but it was too loud."

You can say, "The new family that's coming to our small group seems nice." And they'll say, "Yeah, but their kids get on my nerves."

Yowbutters. Cynics. Pessimists. Call them what you want. They are the rain on your parade. The pinprick in your balloon. The rock in your shoe. The bone in your chicken salad. They will point out problems you never noticed before and make them seem bigger than they really are. They will depress, discourage and demoralize even the most upbeat climbers.

The Critics

Then, of course, there are the critics. They are a little different breed of naysayer, but equally as dangerous. They generally come on like gangbusters. They have strong personalities and even stronger opinions. They're not opposed to climbing. In fact, often they will be climbers themselves. But they believe *their* way of climbing is better than *your* way of climbing, and they don't hesitate to let you know it.

I once attended the funeral of a person who was killed in a fire. I assumed the body would be horribly disfigured and walked in expecting the casket to be closed. It was open, however, and the deceased person looked perfectly normal. Cornering the funeral director, I asked if the person had been burned on parts of his body that were not visible. "No," he said, "the man doesn't have a mark on him. He was killed by the smoke, not the flames." Since then I have learned that four out of five people who die in fires are killed by smoke inhalation.

Harsh, unjust criticism is like smoke. It doesn't leave welts or bruises. It doesn't require stitches or bandages. It doesn't leave a person mangled or disfigured. But it can choke the life right out of him. That's why James said that the tongue "is an uncontrollable evil, full of deadly poison. Sometimes it praises our Lord and Father, and sometimes it breaks out into curses against those who have been made in the image of God. And so blessing and cursing come pouring out of the same mouth. Surely, my brothers and sisters, *this is not right!*" (James 3:8b–10, author's emphasis).

When you encounter cynics and critics on the mountain of the Lord, there's not much you can do except grit your teeth and keep climbing. As one pastor said, "You can't change them, you can't trade them, and you can't shoot them, so you might as well just ignore them and keep going." That's commitment.

COMMITMENT IS THE SECRET TO OVERCOMING OBSTACLES

Here are three of the more common obstacles climbers on the mountain of the Lord encounter.

Obstacle #1: Adversity

Sometimes an unexpected twist of circumstances can turn your life upside down. A doctor's diagnosis, a lawsuit, divorce papers, unemployment or a sudden disability can cause you to question everything you believe in, especially if you've always been a diligent climber. When disaster strikes, it's so easy to look heavenward and say, "What's up with this, Lord? After all these years of climbing, this is what I get?"

Maybe you're in that situation right now. Maybe your world recently has caved in, and you're having serious doubts about God and His promises. Maybe you're not even sure you want to keep climbing. If so, let me remind you of a couple of simple, but important truths.

First, every climber suffers. It may not be in the same way, but there's not a person on Earth who hasn't experienced some pain and hardship. Read 2 Corinthians 11 and refresh your memory concerning the many hardships Paul faced. Also consider that Jesus, the only perfect man who ever lived, suffered terribly.

Second, giving up your climb won't suddenly end your suffering. I am always amazed at how many climbers abandon their expedition and retreat to the valley at the first sign of hardship, as if the valley is some kind of refuge. Aren't they forgetting why they wanted to get out of the valley in the first place? My observation is that most people who retreat to the valley find *more* suffering, not less. Why? Because, in addition to their current struggle (illness, divorce, unemployment, etc.), they then have the added burden of guilt, knowing in their hearts that they have abandoned the mountain of the Lord.

Let me share with you my favorite verse for times of adversity. It's one that I have read and prayed over in my own hours of darkness, and one that I have shared with countless fellow climbers. It's Psalm 31:7. David said, "I am overcome with joy because of your unfailing love, for you have seen my troubles, and you care about the anguish of my soul." That verse invigorates me in times of trouble like few others I have found. Like David, I find great joy in knowing that God is aware of my troubles and that he cares about my pain. With that assurance, I can recommit myself to His mountain and keep climbing.

Obstacle #2: Abandonment

Climbing is a sport that builds strong relationships. That's because climbers share an intense passion, face unique dangers and are forced to work together in perfect synchronization in order to reach their goals. Like Hillary and Norgay or Mallory and Irvine, many climbers become so closely connected, both personally and professionally, that it's hard to think of one without the other. In such cases, the old saying, "They were made for each other," rings especially true.

Maybe there is a person in your life whom God seems to have made just for you. Perhaps it's your spouse, a lifelong friend or a coworker. No doubt it's someone who understands and appreciates you. Someone who knows what you need, when you need it, and who never fails to deliver right on time. Someone whose strengths and weaknesses mesh perfectly with your own. Such a person can be a delightful climbing partner, one who makes every step a pleasure.

But what do you do when that person is suddenly gone?

In Scripture, Joshua is a good example of a person who lost a cherished climbing partner. Moses was his mentor and friend. He taught Joshua the finer points of military strategy, as well as the nuances of working with people. But most of all, he encouraged the growth and development of Joshua's faith. Deuteronomy 34:9a says, "Now Joshua, son of Nun, was full of the spirit of wisdom, for Moses had laid his hands on him." No wonder Joshua was unshakable in his loyalty to Moses.

But there came a day when Moses died, and Joshua was left to continue climbing without him. Many scholars believe that Joshua was devastated and sank into a state of depression that lasted well beyond the customary thirty-day mourning period. That would explain the rousing pep talk the Lord gave him in Joshua 1:1–9. It was a pep talk in which God commanded Joshua to be strong and courageous, no less than three times (vv. 6, 7, 9). Essentially, he was saying to Joshua, "Moses is gone, and I need you to take over his role. Now is the time to firm up your commitment. We still have a lot of work to do."

Whether by death, relocation or betrayal, being left alone by a cherished climbing partner can be devastating. It's easy to think you'll never again be as happy or as effective in your climbing. You might even wonder if there's any point in continuing to climb, especially if that person was truly the wind beneath your wings, the one who kept you pumped up and motivated. But remember what God said to Joshua: "Do not be afraid or discouraged. For the Lord your God is with you wherever you go" (Josh. 1:9b). Commit yourself to moving forward in spite of your sadness, and you'll discover, like Joshua, that God will cover your loss and provide what you need to continue reaching new heights. He might even provide you with a new climbing partner—another one made just for you.

Obstacle #3: Annoyance

I recently ran across a little book that appropriately was titled *Life's Little Destruction Book*. It was nothing more than a list of suggestions on how to be annoying. For example, you can:

Tell your friends how the movie ends before they go see it.

Use up all the toilet paper without replacing the roll.

Get in the express lane at the supermarket with too many items.

Don't brush your teeth so you'll have bad breath.

Wear a large hat to the movies.

Push all the buttons before exiting an elevator.

Pay highway tolls with one-hundred-dollar bills.

As I was perusing the list, it occurred to me that the world is full of people who do not need any suggestions on how to be annoying. They are just naturally gifted in that area and have mastered the art all by themselves. The problem is, you will occasionally find yourself climbing alongside these people. Maybe at this moment you can name someone in your church who drives you nuts. The person may be a sincere, well-intentioned climber, but simply has a personality that sets your teeth on edge.

READER/CUSTOMER CARE SURVEY

We care about your opinions. Please take a moment to fill out this Reader Survey card and mail it back to us.
As a special **"thank you"** we'll send you exciting news about interesting books and a valuable **Gift Certificate.**

Please PRINT using ALL CAPS

First Name |_____| MI. |__| Last Name |_____|

Address |_____|

City |_____| ST |___| Zip |_____| — |____|

Phone # (|___|) |____| — |____| Fax # (|___|) |____| — |____|

Email |_____|

(1) Gender:

_____ Female   _____ Male

(2) Age:

_____ 12 or under   _____ 40-59

_____ 13-19   _____ 60+

_____ 20-39

(3) Marital Status

_____ Married

_____ Single

_____ Divorced/Widowed

(4) Did you receive this book as a gift?

_____ Yes   _____ No

(6) How did you find out about this book?
Please fill in ONE.

1) _____ Recommendation

2) _____ Store Display

3) _____ Bestseller List

4) _____ Online

5) _____ Advertisement

6) _____ Catalog/Mailing

7) _____ Interview/Review (TV, Radio, Print)

(7) Where do you usually buy books?
Please fill in your top TWO choices.

1) _____ General Bookstore

2) _____ Christian Bookstore

3) _____ Online

4) _____ Book Club/Mail Order

5) _____ Price Club (Costco, Sam's Club, etc.)

6) _____ Retail Store (Target, Wal-Mart, etc.)

(9) What subjects do you enjoy reading about most? Rank only *FIVE.* *Use 1 for your favorite, 2 for second favorite, etc.*

	1	2	3	4	5
1) Parenting/Family	O	O	O	O	O
2) Relationships	O	O	O	O	O
3) Recovery/Addictions	O	O	O	O	O
4) Health/Nutrition	O	O	O	O	O
5) Christian Living	O	O	O	O	O
6) Inspiration	O	O	O	O	O
7) Business Self-Help	O	O	O	O	O
8) Teen Issues	O	O	O	O	O
9) Sports	O	O	O	O	O

(14) What attracts you most to a book?
(Please rank 1-4 in order of preference.)

	1	2	3	4
1) Title	O	O	O	O
2) Cover Design	O	O	O	O
3) Author	O	O	O	O
4) Content	O	O	O	O

TAPE IN MIDDLE; DO NOT STAPLE

BUSINESS REPLY MAIL

FIRST-CLASS MAIL PERMIT NO 45 DEERFIELD BEACH, FL

POSTAGE WILL BE PAID BY ADDRESSEE

FAITH COMMUNICATIONS
3201 SW 15TH STREET
DEERFIELD BEACH FL 33442-9875

FOLD HERE

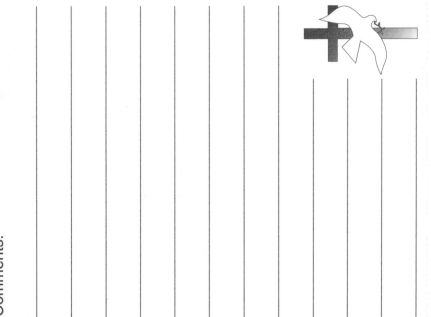

Comments:

I have known very few climbers who have retreated to the valley because of annoying people they've met on the mountain, but I've known a lot of climbers who have jumped from one expedition to another in search of climbers who possess no flaws. That, it seems to me, is the great danger here. Sometimes a person joins an expedition with unrealistic expectations, thinking that every member is going to be a joy to climb with. Then, when that turns out not to be the case, they become disgruntled.

The truth is that we all have two IQs. We all have an Intelligence Quotient and an *Irritation* Quotient. Yes, even you, my friend. Trust me. Even as you are reading these words, there is someone in this world who thinks you are annoying. The problem is, although we all can be irritating to others, we seldom spot those irritating traits in ourselves. John C. Maxwell nails the truth of the matter in his book *Becoming a Person of Influence.*[1]

When the other fellow takes a long time, he's slow.
When I take a long time, I'm thorough.

When the other fellow doesn't do it, he's lazy.
When I don't do it, I'm busy.

When the other fellow charges ahead, he's overstepping his bounds.
When I charge ahead, I'm taking initiative.

---

[1] John Maxwell, *Becoming a Person of Influence,* (Nashville: Thomas Nelson, 1997), 113.

When the other fellow pleases the boss, he's an apple polisher.

When I please the boss, I'm cooperating.

When the other fellow forgets a rule of etiquette, he's rude.

When I forget a rule of etiquette, I'm in a hurry.

When the other fellow is successful, he's lucky.

When I am successful, I'm diligent.

God apparently knew we would get on each other's nerves. That's why the Bible contains so many exhortations to be loving and tolerant.

> Love each other with genuine affection, and take delight in honoring each other. (Rom. 12:10)
>
> Let us aim for harmony in the church and try to build each other up. (Rom. 14:19)
>
> Accept each other just as Christ has accepted you. (Rom. 15:7)
>
> Love is patient and kind. (1 Cor. 13:4)
>
> Dear children, let us stop just saying we love each other; let us really show it by our actions. (1 John 3:18)
>
> Be kind to each other, tenderhearted, forgiving one another, *just as God through Christ has forgiven you.* (Eph. 4:32, author's emphasis)

Get the picture? The question is not, will you encounter fellow climbers who annoy you? The question is, how will you react when you do? Again, it all boils down to commitment. If you're committed to climbing and to loving your fellow climbers the way God has loved you, you'll be fine.

Wrapping up this chapter on commitment, I want to tell you about a magazine ad I'm looking at. It's in the current issue of *Rock & Ice,* and I have to tell you, it stopped me cold. Patagonia, a company that sells top-of-the-line outdoor apparel, has a simple, but effective slogan: "Committed to the Core." In this ad they have pictured a man's hands folded one on top of the other, and what a mess they are. The hands are dirty, scratched, scarred and missing chunks of flesh. The fingernails are cracked and chipped. The cuticles are torn, and there are numerous scabs. A climber whose hands are in this condition is said to have had an "alpine manicure."

The message of the ad is clear. These are the hands of a climber who is "committed to the core." The picture reminds me of Paul's statement: "I bear on my body the scars that show I belong to Jesus" (Gal. 6:17b).

My prayer is that all of us who are climbing the mountain of the Lord would be so committed to the Rock of Ages that no opponent or obstacle would be able to turn us away from the summit.

Seven

BUILD UP YOUR
INTEGRITY

*"Climbing is, above all, a
matter of integrity."*

—Gaston Rebufat

In Psalm 24:4, David lists the third requirement for anyone who wishes to climb the mountain of the Lord. He says
that such a person must "never tell lies." In other words, he
must be completely devoted to the truth. He must deliver on
his promises. He must be a person of absolute integrity.

Like Rob Hall.

Rob was one of the world's premier mountaineers and
the co-owner of Adventure Consultants, a guide service that
took wealthy clients to the top of the world's tallest mountains. For a mere sixty-five thousand dollars, Rob would take

his customers anywhere in the world and personally escort them up and down the monster mountain of their choice.

In May 1996, he was leading an expedition of eight climbers to the top of Mt. Everest. They were well trained and well equipped. The weather was perfect, and no problems were anticipated. In fact, several other expeditions were on the mountain at the same time, and more than thirty climbers were expected to reach the summit on the same day.

But as one climber later observed, that day the mountain was hungry.

Out of nowhere, a ferocious storm swept across the notorious "Death Zone" with snow, sub-zero temperatures and hurricane-force winds. The storm caught the climbers as they were descending and showed no mercy. One climber, a postal worker from Kent, Washington, named Doug Hansen, was overcome by the elements and collapsed. It was apparent that he would not be able to make it back to camp and would be dead in a matter of hours. At that point, Rob Hall, who was still in good condition, had a decision to make. Would he head back to camp and leave his suffering client to die alone in the snow? Or would he stay by Hansen's side to the bitter end, thus endangering his own life?

Rob Hall decided to stay with his client, and his logic was simple. He had made a promise to his clients that he would take them up *and down* the mountain. Rob believed that leaving Doug Hansen to die would make him a fraud. Never again would anyone trust him. His reputation would be permanently damaged. So in his mind there was really no choice at all. He *had* to stay with his client, even if it meant facing death himself.

In just a few hours, Doug Hansen was dead, but by then Rob Hall was too weak to walk. At 4:35 A.M., while he still had enough strength to speak, he called the camp on his two-way radio and asked to be patched through to his wife, Dr. Jan Arnold, who was back in New Zealand and seven months pregnant with their first child. They talked as his life slipped away. His last words to his wife were, "I love you. Sleep well, my sweetheart. Please don't worry too much." And then he was heard quietly weeping. He didn't realize his radio was still on.

In all, eight of the more than thirty climbers died on Everest that day, and several others ended up with life-threatening injuries. Rob Hall's body was recovered the following afternoon and dropped down a crevasse, which is the traditional form of burial for climbers who die on mountains. Although many think he was crazy for not saving himself, he will long be remembered as a man who chose to die rather than go back on his word.

My dictionary defines integrity simply as "personal honesty." Even more revealing is the word's middle English root, which means "to integrate" or "to bring together as a whole." The idea is that personal honesty should be something that ties every aspect of your life together. Whether you're in negotiations with a client, reasoning with one of your children, playing golf with your buddies or leading an expedition up

Mt. Everest, you should be recognized as a person who tells the truth and keeps promises.

Unfortunately, integrity seems to be harder and harder to find in our culture. In recent years, we have seen a U.S. president playing silly word games to try to hide the truth about an illicit affair. We've seen CIA employees selling secrets to foreign governments and tire manufacturers covering up information about defective products. We've seen a U.S. congressman in a shady, secret relationship with a woman half his age (who mysteriously vanished and later was found dead). We've seen major college football coaches lying about their credentials. We've seen corporate executives looting their companies and ripping off their employees. And we've seen a parade of well-respected superstar athletes being charged with everything from sexual assault to murder. Clearly, we live in an age of deceit and hypocrisy. So extreme is our culture's integrity crisis that many people find it hard to trust anyone they don't know. We think every solicitation is a scam, every salesman is a con artist, every politician is a crook, every lawyer is an ambulance chaser, and every television evangelist is a charlatan.

I'd love to be able to say that the church is an oasis of integrity in this desert of dishonesty, but I can't. Churchgoers may not be as extreme in their dishonesty as some of the crooks who live to rip people off, but there's still more dishonesty in the church than there should be. I've seen it in four main areas.

Church people often misrepresent how *holy* they are.

How *humble* they are.

How *hungry* they are.

And how *happy* they are.

I'm not suggesting that the church is full of liars and crooks, although every church probably has a few. I'm simply suggesting that a lot of Christians are reluctant to show who they really are, usually for fear of rejection. We tend to go underground with our weaknesses and pretend to be better than we really are.

Just three days ago, I walked into a convenience store to buy a newspaper. I paid my fifty-four cents and was heading for the door when I heard somebody say in a soft, but urgent tone of voice, "Oh no, it's the preacher!" I looked back and saw two people from my church standing at the Lotto machine with a fistful of tickets. I hadn't noticed them before. The man offered a friendly hello, but the woman couldn't have looked more guilty if she'd been holding a bloody knife. "You caught us," she said. To which her husband quickly responded, "*Us!* You mean he caught *you! You're* the one who always wants to buy these tickets!" The truth is, I didn't *catch* either of them. I would have walked out the door without even seeing them if the woman's guilty conscience hadn't caused her to speak out.

You see, integrity involves more than being honest in a business deal. It involves more than telling the truth under oath in a court of law. It involves more than keeping your promises to your family or your employees. It also involves being honest about who you are. The story of Ananias and Sapphira (Acts 5:1–11) is shocking to some because God struck them dead even though they didn't do anything illegal. However, they did misrepresent themselves, and God considered that to be an offense worthy of death. Clearly, God was trying to impress upon his infant church the importance of integrity.

Think for a moment about the *importance* and the *implementation* of integrity as they relate to climbing the mountain of the Lord.

THE IMPORTANCE OF INTEGRITY

The Bible mentions three wonderful things integrity does for climbers.

First, integrity ENRICHES the climbing experience.

Psalm 119:1 says, "Happy are people of integrity, who follow the law of the Lord." Why are they happy? Because they avoid much of the trouble and stress with which dishonest people have to contend. For example, a person of integrity won't ever get caught in a lie. He won't ever get caught shoplifting or padding his expense account or cheating on his taxes. He won't ever get fired because of laziness. He won't ever feel guilty for cheating a customer. He won't ever get caught kissing another man's wife or renting an X-rated DVD or buying lottery tickets. And, perhaps best of all, he won't have to face the day-to-day pressure of trying to make other people believe he's better than he really is. You show me a person who never has to face any of those pressures, and I'll show you a person who has taken a *giant* step in the direction of happiness.

If your life has become stressful and difficult, maybe you need to ask yourself some hard questions. Are the pressures you're facing self-inflicted? Are they the result of some lapses of integrity? Have you recently compromised some basic conviction that you once held dear? Do you sometimes find yourself doing things that at one time you wouldn't even have considered? Do you find yourself adapting to the integrity level of the people you're with instead of sticking to your guns and always following your conscience?

If your answer is yes to even one of those questions, you may have just discovered the reason for your unhappiness. I challenge you to get busy and reclaim that lost ground. Renew your commitment to absolute honesty in every area of your life, and you'll almost certainly find relief. Remember, we always reap what we sow (Gal. 6:7).

Second, integrity ESTABLISHES firm footing.

Every serious climber knows the importance of good footing. That's why, when you walk into a store that sells climbing shoes, you'll find an Imelda Marcos type of assortment, with many styles costing as much as two hundred dollars. Many novice climbers balk at spending that kind of money on shoes, but one trip to the rock usually changes their minds. After slipping and sliding all over the place, they come down, hustle back to the store and drop the money.

Proverbs 10:9 says, "People with integrity have firm footing, but those who follow crooked paths will slip and fall." In life, there are many places to set your feet. Stepping with integrity will keep you from slipping and embarrassing yourself, or worse yet, ruining your life.

In my lifetime, Billy Graham has been perhaps the greatest example of a sure-footed climber. Some might disagree with his theology, and others might be more gifted in the pulpit, but *no one* has demonstrated greater integrity. In a "business" that often has been manipulated for the preacher's personal gain, and while countless other famous preachers have come under suspicion, Billy Graham has come through unscathed. No slips. No falls. No embarrassments for the kingdom.

You may not be a nationally known figure like Billy Graham, but you still have a sphere of influence. You still have family members and friends, many of whom will be following in your footsteps. That's why it's crucial that you be careful and live with integrity. Not only will you save yourself from a nasty fall, but your example could save your loved ones as well.

Third, integrity EARNS God's protection.

Proverbs 11:8 says, "God rescues the godly from danger, but he lets the wicked fall into trouble." And Proverbs 10:25

says, "Disaster strikes like a cyclone, whirling the wicked away, but the godly have a lasting foundation." Those two verses should get every climber's attention because they each mention something that every climber worries about. The first verse mentions *falling,* and the second verse mentions *bad weather.* The vast majority of history's greatest mountain disasters have involved either a fall or bad weather, and sometimes both.

Former gymnast Beverly Johnson and her partner Dan Asey were climbing Yosemite's El Capitan one day when they were startled by a human body zooming past in the midst of a two-thousand-foot fall. Asey and Johnson stared wide-eyed at each other, swallowed hard and went back to work. Very carefully.

We face similar dangers when climbing the mountain of the Lord. The Bible speaks of the possibility of falling in our walk with the Lord (Jude 24) and also of the storms we will face (Matt. 7:24–27). But the Scripture also promises God's protection to the climber who is "godly." Notice, it doesn't say that the godly climber won't ever encounter a stumbling block or that he won't ever see a cyclone, only that he'll be "rescued" and given a "lasting foundation" when he does.

And speaking of lasting foundations, now is a time when we need one. As I'm writing these words, there is great fear in the hearts of many Americans. The SARS virus is spreading, and there's still no cure. North Korea is threatening to develop and use weapons of mass destruction. Government warnings concerning future terrorist attacks are broadcast on a regular basis. You can't even go to a play or a sporting event without being searched and put through a metal detector. Sometimes it seems as if the whole world is teetering on the edge of a great abyss. In these troubled times, I, for one, am thankful for God's promise to provide the godly with a lasting foundation. As the world destabilizes, I can rest assured that He is still the Solid Rock (Ps. 62:2).

THE IMPLEMENTATION OF INTEGRITY

Understanding the importance of integrity is one thing, but implementing it will always be easier said than done. Why? Because there are so many people who want you to fail. Satan does, obviously. But so do all the people around you who have chosen not to live with integrity. They want you to fail so they can laugh and say, "See, he's no different from the rest of us!"

I love the story of A. C. Green. He was a fine professional basketball player, the NBA's "Iron Man," who played in 1,192 consecutive games. That's over fourteen straight seasons without missing a single contest. But an even more amazing fact about A. C. Green is that he steadfastly maintained his virginity in a business that makes it very easy to be promiscuous. As an outspoken Christian, he has diligently promoted his faith and encouraged young people to have the strength to say no to temptation, holding himself up as a role model, not in an egotistical way, but simply to prove that it can be done.

During his rookie year with the Lakers, several veteran players said that A. C.'s virgin status wouldn't last six weeks. With so much money in his pocket and a beautiful girl never more than five feet away, Mr. Goody Two-Shoes was doomed, they said. But they were wrong. A. C. remained true to his commitment until marrying his dream girl, Veronique, on April 20, 2002. I'm thankful for the A. C. Greens of this world because they prove to all of us that it is possible to live with integrity even in a difficult environment.

There are many strategies a person can employ in the pursuit of integrity. One that has helped me on numerous occasions is based on a simple question and a passage of Scripture. First, the Scripture:

> *M*any *people, including some of the Jewish leaders, believed in him [Jesus]. But they wouldn't admit it to anyone because of their fear that the Pharisees would expel them from the synagogue.* For they loved human praise more than the praise of God. *(John 12:42–43 author's emphasis)*

That's a telling passage, isn't it? It shows what we might call "reverse hypocrisy." Generally, we think of religious hypocrisy as being an unbeliever acting like a believer. But here we have a case of believers acting like unbelievers! Why? Because they craved the approval of men.

So here's the question. The one you must answer before

you'll ever be able to make a firm commitment to integrity:

Whose approval do you crave?

If you crave the approval of men, you'll do whatever it takes to win it.

You'll twist the truth in order to make the sale and impress your boss.

You'll suck up to people who can help you, even if you can't stand them.

You'll exaggerate your successes.

You'll blame others for your failures.

You'll claim to work harder than you really do.

You'll claim to be wealthier than you really are.

You'll tell people what they want to hear rather than what you really think.

You'll learn to hide any weakness or sin that would tarnish your image.

And, of course, you'll pretend to be horrified and disgusted at every breach of integrity you see in others.

At the same time, if you crave the approval of God, you'll also do whatever it takes to win it.

Danny Wuerffel was a record-setting quarterback at the University of Florida. He led the Gators to three straight SEC championships, passed for more than 10,000 yards, threw 114 touchdowns and established an NCAA record with a pass efficiency rating of 163.6. Just prior to his senior year when he won the Heisman Trophy, he was invited to appear in *Playboy* magazine, as a member of the preseason All-America team and the National Scholar Athlete of the Year. The honor included an all-expense-paid trip to a swanky resort in Phoenix and a photo shoot with the twenty-three other players who also were selected.

But Danny Wuerffel declined the offer.

He felt that his appearance in such a magazine would conflict with his testimony as a Christian and possibly mislead some of his fans. Although others thought he was crazy, he didn't care. He was more concerned about God's approval than the world's.

You may not be a superstar quarterback who has the world beating a path to your door, but you will still face many moments—probably one or two every day—when you will have to choose between the world's approval and God's. There's no getting around it. Those are the moments when your integrity will be made or broken.

And consider this.

Life in our world is lived at warp speed. These "moments of truth" will come flying at you out of nowhere when you least expect them. You may not have time to sit down and think things through. You may not have time to weigh the pros and cons of your decision. That's why it's absolutely imperative that you make your choice ahead of time. Walk into any school or hospital, and you'll see an evacuation plan posted on the wall as well as lighted "exit" signs. That means somebody has already made the decision of what to do *before* the fire breaks out. It would be disastrous to wait until the hallways were filled with smoke before coming up with a plan of action.

Whose approval do you crave?

That's the question you must answer, and right now is the time to answer it.

Keep in mind that it's never too late to start living with integrity. In Scripture, Zacchaeus is a good example of a guy who lived for years as a crook, but turned his life around before it was too late (Luke 19:1–10). If you've been less than honest in your business, with your spouse or in your personal finances, go back and read his story. Notice how Jesus singled him out of the crowd. That means Jesus knew his heart, just like he knows yours. And notice how gracious Jesus was when he saw that Zacchaeus's repentance was genuine. That same grace is awaiting you, my friend, when you decide to repent and pursue absolute honesty in every area of your life.

Part Three:

THE PANORAMA

When through the woods and forest glades I wander
And hear the birds sing sweetly in the trees
When I look down from lofty mountain grandeur
And hear the brook, and feel the gentle breeze
Then sings my soul, my Savior God, to Thee
How great Thou art
How great Thou art

Stuart K. Hine,
"How Great Thou Art," 1941

Eight

SOAK UP YOUR BLESSINGS

*"To those who have struggled with them,
the mountains reveal beauties that they will not
disclose to those who have made no effort."*

—Sir Francis Younghusband

Many people say that Beck Weathers is a living, breathing miracle, and I wouldn't want to argue the point. As a forty-nine-year-old amateur climber and full-time pathologist, he joined the Rob Hall expedition that I described at the beginning of the last chapter. With his marriage in shambles, his professional life in high gear and his stress level off the charts, he thought a trek to the top of Mt. Everest would satisfy some inner longing and bring him the peace that had been eluding him for so long.

But the mountain had other ideas.

Well short of the summit, Weathers realized he was in trouble. Partial blindness had set in, caused by the high altitude, so he informed Rob Hall that he couldn't go on. At that point, only one course of action made any sense. Hall instructed Weathers to wait at that spot. The expedition would continue on to the summit and pick him up on the way down. Weathers never dreamed that a world-class climber and guide like Rob Hall would die higher up and never make it back.

Eventually realizing that he was stranded, Weathers joined up with another expedition that happened to be passing by on its way down. Tied to the others by a rope, Weathers trudged through the snow, staggering and feeling his way, but getting closer to safety with every step.

And then the storm hit.

Some said it sounded like a low-pitched growl coming up the mountain and then simply exploded all around them. In seconds, the temperature dropped to sixty degrees below zero, and the wind hit seventy miles an hour. The snow was so intense that visibility dropped to less than a foot. One climber said it was like being trapped in a bottle of milk.

In such extreme conditions, the weaker climbers simply were unable to keep going, so Weathers and a few others were left behind as the stronger climbers went for help. They lay down next to each other and did whatever they could to keep each other awake. They yelled and kicked and shook each other, realizing that sleep was their deadliest enemy. But inevitably, exhaustion set in. Their limbs soon felt as heavy as lead, and their voices were gone. With nothing left to give and feeling numb from head to toe, they closed their eyes and drifted off to sleep.

The next morning, after the storm had passed, a small expedition began searching for Weathers and his friends and found them half-buried in the snow. Stuart Hutchinson, a cardiologist, was leading the expedition and realized that Weathers was in a hypothermic coma. Understanding that hypothermic comas are always fatal at such extreme altitudes, Hutchinson made the decision not to endanger more lives by trying to get the bodies back to camp. So, for the third time, Beck Weathers was left behind.

That he eventually woke up and was clearheaded enough to assess his situation is, many say, a miracle. Half-buried in the snow, his hands and face were frozen, but his mind was alive and working. He pictured his family back home in Texas. He saw his wife, Peach, with whom he'd been fighting for so long and thought about the fact that he hadn't really said good-bye. Hadn't told her he loved her. Hadn't tried—*really* tried—to make things right.

And that's when he decided to go home.

Somehow Weathers got to his feet and started walking. When he staggered into camp with a Frankenstein-like stiffness to his gait and his face and hands frozen and horribly disfigured, he looked like something out of a cheap horror film. Those in camp couldn't believe their eyes. They'd heard that Weathers was dead and had even called his wife in Texas and told her that he had perished in the storm. But there he was—alive, if not well—a man that eternity simply refused to accept.

Weathers's recovery was long and difficult. Both his hands and his nose were amputated and either reconstructed or replaced with a prosthetic. Today, he still practices medicine and travels the country giving motivational speeches and answering questions about his ordeal. He says that the most intriguing question he's ever been asked is this: "If you could do it all over again, knowing what was going to happen, would you?" Believe it or not, his answer is "yes." Why? Because, as he loves to point out, "I gained so much more than I lost."

Throughout this book, I've stressed that climbing the mountain of the Lord is difficult. You *will* encounter hardship. You *will* be called upon to make some sacrifices. You *will* lose a few things along the way. But the promise of the Bible is that you'll gain a lot more than you'll lose. David says that those who climb the mountain of the Lord "will receive the Lord's blessing and have right standing with God their savior" (Ps. 24:5).

In chapter 1 of this book, I mentioned four of the treasures (blessings) that climbers will find on the mountain of the Lord. In this chapter, I want to talk about the greatest blessing of all, that of being right with God. For the Christian, *that* is the summit. The preeminent desire. The ultimate goal.

What Being Right with God Doesn't Mean

While the *importance* of being right with God cannot be overestimated, the *meaning* of it certainly can. Let me mention a few facts you should keep in mind.

Fact #1: Being right with God doesn't mean you're done climbing.

When Paul wrote the book of Philippians, he certainly was right with God, but he was far from finished as a climber. He said, "I don't mean to say that I have already achieved these things or that I have already reached perfection! But I keep working toward that day when I will finally be all that Christ has saved me for and wants me to be. No, dear brothers and sisters, I am still not all I should be, but I am focusing all my energies on this one thing: Forgetting the past and looking forward to what lies ahead, I strain to reach the end of the race and receive the prize for which God, through Christ Jesus, is calling us up to heaven" (Phil. 3:12–14). This passage proves that as long as we draw breath there will be old habits to fight, new truths to learn and new ridges to conquer.

Not long ago, I knocked on the door of an eighty-something-year-old woman and found her sitting at her kitchen table with her Bible and a scribbled-up yellow notepad. She had been studying and couldn't wait to tell me about a nugget of truth she'd just uncovered. I was heartened to see that even with a million steps behind her and a body battered by time, she was still climbing.

If you're a veteran climber on the mountain of the Lord, understand that the greatest treasures of all may still be ahead of you, just over the next ridge. That possibility is what drove Ben Merold to become the senior minister of the Harvester Christian Church in St. Charles, Missouri, at the age of sixty-four. At a time when most people are looking for a rocking chair, he was looking for a challenge. And God has blessed both Ben and the church. That congregation, which had an average Sunday morning attendance of about two hundred when Ben took over, is now running over three thousand. Ben has been there just over twelve years and shows no signs of stopping. Who knows what God may yet do through such a willing climber!

Fact #2: Being right with God doesn't mean Satan has given up on you.

I saw a *Far Side* cartoon one time that showed two deer standing in the woods. One of the deer had a marking on his chest that looked like a big target. The other deer simply said, "Bummer of a birthmark, Hal."

If you're a veteran climber on the mountain of the Lord, you have a target on your chest. Satan is coming after you. He loves nothing more than to cause people like you to stumble. One reason is because it gives him an opportunity to laugh at God and say, "Gotcha!" But it's also a way to spread pain, heartache and discouragement throughout the body of Christ. Paul understood this. That's why he said, "I run straight to the goal with purpose in every step. I am not like a boxer who misses his punches. I discipline my body like an athlete, training it to do what it should. Otherwise, I fear that after preaching to others I myself might be disqualified" (1 Cor. 9:26–27).

A veteran climber once said to me, "The devil's not welcome in my home, but he's camped in my front yard just waiting for me to step outside." It's a wise man who recognizes the persistence of Satan. Although his defeat already has been accomplished, he's going to go down swinging.

Fact #3: Being right with God doesn't mean an end to suffering.

When the twin towers of the World Trade Center came crashing down, believers died right alongside unbelievers. I read about one lady who wandered the streets of New York for days, clutching a picture of her missing husband and showing it to everyone she met. Her husband worked in one of the towers, but had been taking night classes with the hope of becoming a preacher. His body eventually was pulled from the rubble.

James 1:2 says, "Dear brothers and sisters, whenever trouble comes your way, let it be an opportunity for joy." Notice, he doesn't say "*if* trouble comes your way," but "*whenever* trouble comes your way." There's no discussion of the probability. It's simply a foregone conclusion that trouble *will* come.

David Jeremiah is an outstanding preacher and bestselling author who discovered in 1994 that he had lymphoma, a dangerous form of cancer that attacks the spleen. In his book, *A Bend in the Road,* which chronicles his fight against the deadly disease, he strikes at the heart of the issue:

> We Christians have no immunity whatsoever to pain or suffering. It matters not whether you're a new convert or a spiritual giant, you're still an imperfect human creature living in a fallen world; you struggle with all the blessings and burdens being a member of the family of man entails. When we become part of God's own family, what sets us apart is not any difference in the sin environment around us, but in how we deal with it.

That's not great news, is it? In fact, I suspect you might even feel a little discouraged at this point. Realizing that we will always have climbing to do, that Satan will never leave us alone, and that suffering will always be a part of life's equation easily could make you want to throw up your hands and say, "What's the use!"

But hold on, my friend. Here comes the good news!

WHAT BEING RIGHT WITH GOD *DOES* MEAN

Here are three facts to balance out the ones we just considered.

Fact #1: Being right with God means you have a FAITHFUL FRIEND.

Earlier this year, a man was found dead in his Orlando home. He'd been shot in the chest and left sprawled on his living-room floor. Because his house was ransacked and a few valuables were missing, it was assumed that he'd walked in on an armed robber and suffered the consequences. However, the investigation revealed that the ransacking and the stealing were just a cover. The man actually had been killed by his next-door neighbor. The victim's mother was quoted as saying that the two men had been best friends since childhood.

In this world, friendships often die. Sometimes they wither away from a lack of attention, and sometimes they explode in anger and violence. Right now, I'm sure you could name several people you once counted as close friends, but do no longer. I'm sure you also could tell at least one horror story about how you were betrayed by a friend. I know some people who have been burned so many times that they have practically withdrawn from the human race. They would rather be lonely than risk being hurt again.

One of the greatest blessings of being right with God is that you have a faithful friend in Jesus. In John 15:14–15 he said, "You are my friends if you obey me. I no longer call you servants, because a master doesn't confide in his servants. Now you are my friends. . . ." And in Matthew 28:20b he said, "Be sure of this: I am with you always, even to the end of the age."

Everybody likes to have a powerful and important friend. Right now, think of someone famous with whom you'd like to be friends . . . maybe a longtime hero, someone whose work you have enjoyed or who has inspired you. Now ask yourself this question: How much cooler would it be to be friends with the one who made that person? Dear reader, that celebrity you just thought of probably couldn't care less about you, but it should thrill you down to your socks to know that the Creator and Lord of the universe wants to be *your* friend!

But be warned: Friendship with Jesus isn't always easy. Just ask Peter. There were occasions when Jesus pinned his ears back, once even calling him "Satan" (Matt. 16:23). And there were other times when Jesus shot down his boastful assertions like hot-air balloons, making him look foolish in the process (Luke 22:33–34). But these things were never done in a mean-spirited way. Instead, Jesus was merely whittling away Peter's rough edges and turning him into an effective servant-leader for the church he intended to build.

The point is, Jesus is a faithful friend, but He's not a spine-less one. He will love you, but He will also push you to keep climbing. I don't know about you, but that's the kind of friend I both want *and* need. On my own, I might grow discouraged and be tempted to quit. But with my best friend beside me, cheering, pushing and coaching, I feel certain I can reach heights that would otherwise be unthinkable.

Fact #2: Being right with God means you have a FIRM FOUNDATION.

For several years, Marilyn and I lived in the Midwest, right on top of the New Madrid Earthquake Fault. In fact, we lived less than twenty miles from New Madrid, Missouri, the town that gives the fault its name. About once a year, there would be a long article in the local paper, speculating about the timing and the results of what surely would be "the big one." It was coming soon, they said, and when it did our homes would be destroyed and possibly under water. Talk about nerve-wracking! I remember reading those articles and then feeling like I needed to tiptoe across my yard—anything to keep from upsetting the delicate balance beneath my feet!

Foundations are important. Jesus said it well in Matthew 7:24–27 when He told a parable about two men who built houses. One built on sand; the other built on rock. Both houses may have been beautiful. In fact, the house on the sand may have been the most beautiful. But take it from a Florida resident—beauty matters little when your house is sitting in the path of a hurricane. All you want to know is that it's well built and resting on a solid foundation.

The second great blessing of being right with God is that you have a firm foundation to build your life on. No matter what happens, you cannot be overwhelmed. David said it best in Psalm 18:31b–33: "Who but our God is a solid rock? God arms me with strength; he has made my way safe. He makes me as surefooted as a deer, *leading me safely along the mountain heights*" (author's emphasis).

One of my favorite stories in the Bible is about Paul and Silas, a couple of great climbers who were thrown into prison (Acts 16:16–40). They were arrested on a bogus charge, beaten and put in chains. I can just imagine that happening to someone today. The ACLU would go nuts! But no one went nuts for Paul and Silas. No team of high-powered attorneys came rushing to their defense. No CNN reporters set up a remote broadcast site outside their prison cell. To put it mildly, they were in a whole heap of trouble.

How, then, do you explain their little impromptu worship service? How do you explain the fact that those dark prison walls echoed with the sounds of their prayers and praise choruses? Simple. They were right with God, and they knew it. They had taken pains to build their lives on a foundation that couldn't be shaken. They knew that the worst those authorities could do to them would only hasten their reward. Who knows? Maybe they thought they were going to heaven that very night and were celebrating!

A story like this takes on new meaning when jet airplanes start slamming into skyscrapers. Or schoolchildren open fire on their classmates with machine guns. Or your husband walks in and tells you he doesn't love you anymore. That's when it's comforting to know that there is at least one thing in this world you can depend on. If you're right with God, then no matter what happens, you can say with David, "I wait quietly before God, for my salvation comes from him. He alone is my rock and my salvation, my fortress *where I will never be shaken*" (Ps. 62:1–2, author's emphasis).

Fact #3: Being right with God means you have a FABULOUS FUTURE.

Hebrews 11 is one of the most important chapters in the Bible, not so much for its theology, but for the encouragement it offers. It is truly The Climbing Hall of Fame. It names a lot of people who reached great heights on the mountain of the Lord and talks about some of the hardships they faced. In verses 35b–38, the reading gets pretty heavy.

But others trusted God and were tortured, preferring to die rather than turn from God and be free. They placed their hope in the resurrection to a better life. Some were mocked, and their backs were cut open with whips. Others were chained in dungeons. Some died by stoning, and some were sawed in half; others were killed with the sword. Some went about in skins of sheep and goats, hungry and oppressed and mistreated. They were too good for this world. They wandered over deserts and mountains, hiding in caves and holes in the ground.

It's hard for me to read that passage without getting a lump in my throat. When I think about how easy I have it in twenty-first-century America compared to what my spiritual ancestors had to face, I am truly humbled and filled with awe. Many surely would wonder where those people got their strength. What was the secret of their faithfulness?

Look at the passage again.

Read it slowly.

The secret is right there before your eyes.

Do you see it?

It's in the last half of verse 35. It says, "They placed their hope in the resurrection to a better life." In other words, they understood that because they were right with God, they had a fabulous future. Hebrews 11:16a says, "They were looking for a better place, a heavenly homeland."

Mark it down. One of the great secrets of effective climbing is to keep your eyes on eternity. Paul said, "Since you have been raised to new life with Christ, set your sights on the realities of heaven, where Christ sits at God's right hand in the place of honor and power. Let heaven fill your thoughts. Do not think only about things down here on earth" (Col. 3:1–2).

Years ago, I knew a fine Christian lady who took that passage to heart. She had terminal cancer, but never allowed it to poison her spirit. Every time I visited her she talked about heaven and expressed a specific wish. She said, "I'm gonna get me a skateboard and have some fun on those streets of gold!" She'd always been large and, by her own admission, very clumsy. But she would sit and watch her grandkids on their skateboards, thinking it looked like such fun. She used to say,

"When I get my new little petite, athletic body, I'm gonna show those kids how it's done!"

I don't know if there will be skateboards in heaven, and truthfully, I don't think she was really planning on it. I just think she liked talking about it. It was her way of lifting her eyes from the things of this world. It was a tool she used to direct every conversation toward heaven. Even with cancer chewing up her liver, she knew she had a fabulous future.

* * *

A few years ago, a newspaper conducted a search for the happiest person on Earth. Readers were invited to write a short essay, explaining why they were so happy, and mail it in. Some of the more interesting and oddball entries were published.

"I recently won the lottery...."

"I just divorced my idiot husband...."

"I'm marrying a former *Playboy* bunny...."

"My boss just got canned...."

"I'm pregnant...."

"I found out I *don't* have cancer...."

But there was one response that caught my eye. It was different from all the rest. It simply said:

"Jesus loves me."

That entry didn't win, of course. But it did make me, and I'm sure a lot of other people, stop and think.

Three little words.

Just twelve letters and a period.

They don't say much. But then again, they say everything.

They say that I have a faithful friend.

A firm foundation.

And a fabulous future.

And so do you, if you're right with God.

Nine

OFFER UP YOUR WORSHIP

*"Canyons will forever echo with the
joyful cries of those who finally
made it to the top."*

—Rob Hall

In the introduction of this book, I compared Psalm 24:3–6 to a masterwork of art that needed to be brought down out of the attic and hung on the wall for everyone to see. Having dabbled in art, I know there comes a point in the painting process when a picture is almost done, but it needs just the right finishing touch to make it complete. As David composed this beautiful passage, he could have stopped after verse 5 and none of us would have felt slighted. But his final brushstroke in verse 6 makes the picture even more compelling. After describing those who may climb the mountain of the Lord and promising them right standing with God, he says, "They alone may enter God's presence and worship the God of Israel."

The word "worship" literally means "to declare worth." That means every person alive is a worshiper because, by our words and actions, we all declare someone or something to be of supreme worth. For the unbeliever it could be money, power, pleasure, self or any one of a thousand other things. But for the Christian, it's God.

So you can see David's reasoning in verse 5. He figures that if you have...

lifted up your eyes,

girded up your mind,

joined up with an expedition,

gathered up your gear,

cleaned up your life,

firmed up your commitment,

built up your integrity,

and are soaking up blessings,

then God must be what is of supreme worth to you. That's why His language so clearly presents worship as a privilege rather than an obligation. He's not saying that a climber *has* to worship, but that he *gets* to worship! It's the same elevated view of worship that prompted David to confess, "I was glad when they said to me, 'Let us go to the house of the Lord'" (Ps. 122:1).

Jesus also had a high view of worship. One day, He stopped to visit His friends, Mary and Martha (Luke 10:38–42), and found them in very different moods. Mary was content to sit at His feet while Martha was stressing out in the kitchen and complaining because her sister wouldn't get up and help. Our Lord's response was kind, but firm. He said, "My dear Martha, you are so upset over all these details! *There is really only one thing worth being concerned about.* Mary has discovered it—and I won't take it away from her" (author's emphasis).

Unfortunately, worship in our generation has become a springboard for conflict and controversy. No issue in the last twenty years has so aroused the ire of God's people. Those who prefer a contemporary style of worship are advancing like a mighty army on those who prefer a traditional approach. As their ranks swell with the influx of younger, more progressive believers, they're taking ground inch by inch. But the traditionalists aren't going down without a struggle, and in some instances the struggle has turned very ugly. Feelings have been hurt, generations have been turned against each other, and congregations large and small have been torn apart. I'm sure David would be sickened to see how this beautiful privilege that should be our most unifying experience has become our most divisive issue.

Now more than ever, I believe we need to lay down our weapons and pick up our Bibles. We need to rediscover seven biblical truths about worship that transcend issues of style and personal preference. I believe they are the qualities that make our worship pleasing to God and the ones we ought to be pursuing.

GOD IS PLEASED WHEN OUR WORSHIP IS FOCUSED

Focused on him, that is. The second of the Ten Commandments says, "Do not worship any other gods besides Me. Do not make idols of any kind, whether in the shape of birds or animals or fish. You must never worship or bow down to them, for I, the Lord your God, am a jealous God who will not share your affection with any other god!" (Exod. 20:3–5a).

I would guess that you don't have a shrine set up in your home where you bow down to a statue of a cow or a large-mouth bass, but that doesn't necessarily mean your focus in worship hasn't drifted away from the Lord. Some people are more committed to their church, their preacher or their religious heritage than they are to God. And, as stated above, I believe there are a few people who even worship *worship*. In other words, they're so staunchly committed to promoting their style preferences and building the perfect "experience," that they have lost all consideration for the feelings of others and the overall health of the body of Christ.

How long has it been since you stopped to think about just who or what you're worshiping? A lot of people assume that because they go to church on a regular basis, they must be worshiping God. But let me remind you that Jesus condemned a lot of very religious people who were temple regulars. He said, "These people honor me with their lips, but their hearts are far away" (Matt. 15:8).

Where is your heart right now?

GOD IS PLEASED WHEN OUR WORSHIP IS FERVENT

Deep in the Old Testament we find the story of how Asa, the king of Judah, ignited a revival in the land. After hearing a special message from the prophet, Azariah, he had all the idols removed from the land and repaired the altar of the Lord. Then he gathered all the people together for a gigantic worship service. They sacrificed seven hundred oxen and seven thousand sheep and goats. But it's what happened next that I want you to see:

They entered into a covenant to seek the Lord, the God of their ancestors, with all their heart and soul. They agreed that anyone who refused to seek the Lord, the God of Israel, would be put to death—whether young or old, man or woman. They shouted out their oath of loyalty to the Lord with trumpets blaring and horns sounding. All were happy about this covenant, for they had entered into it with all their hearts. Eagerly they sought after God, and they found him. And the Lord gave them rest from their enemies on every side. (2 Chron. 15:12–15)

It's hard to imagine a group of people being more fervent in their worship. Imagine a congregation today proposing a resolution to put to death any person in the church who failed to seek the Lord with all his heart. And then imagine that resolution passing unanimously! (Could there ever be a better time to take up an offering?)

But seriously, that would be the ultimate example of fervent worship. And notice how the Lord responded. It says, "Eagerly they sought after God, and they found him. And the Lord gave them rest from their enemies on every side." God is pleased when our worship is fervent.

Think about that the next time you go to church. Are you one of those people who always sits near the exit so you can make a speedy getaway? Do you collapse into your seat and hunker down like you're there to take a nap? Do you mumble your way through the song service? Do you clip your nails, count ceiling tiles, read your bulletin or check out that pretty redhead in the choir during the sermon? And do you get irritated if the service runs a little long?

The age-old complaint of countless churchgoers is that they don't get anything out of the service. In many cases, it's because they don't put anything into it. God simply doesn't respond when we're just going through the motions. He only responds to fervent, heartfelt worship.

GOD IS PLEASED WHEN
OUR WORSHIP IS FITTING

If ever there was a messed-up church, it was the Corinthian church of the first century. It had many problems, but two in particular were turning their corporate worship times into a circus. First, people were disrupting the service by blurting out "ecstatic utterances" whenever they felt like it. And second, the communion service had become a wild party where some people were getting stuffed and drunk, while others were being completely left out. Paul's assessment of the situation was blunt. He said, "It sounds as if more harm than good is done when you meet together" (1 Cor. 11:17b). It's no wonder, then, that Paul issued the following command: "Be sure that everything is done properly and in order" (1 Cor. 14:40).

I've never been in a church where people got drunk at communion time, but I have seen people speak out of turn. I've heard babies scream and watched children run up and down the aisles during the sermon. I've had my ears tortured by horrendous singers, and I've heard preachers who obviously were not well-prepared try to bluff their way through a sermon. I've visited many churches where *nothing* was done properly and *nothing* was done in order, which is bad enough, of course. But the greater tragedy is that in many of those cases, nobody seemed to mind!

Except God. Remember, Paul said, "God is not a God of disorder, but of peace" (1 Cor. 14:33a).

Sometimes Christians try to shrug off their shoddiness by saying, "We're not professionals, you know. We're just humble Christians making our joyful noise." But whatever happened to giving your best to the Master? You don't have to be a ministry professional to spend some time in preparation. You don't have to be a ministry professional to get yourself organized. You don't have to be a ministry professional to take your crying baby out of the service so others can concentrate. It's all just a matter of doing only those things that are fitting and that show proper respect for God and humanity.

GOD IS PLEASED WHEN OUR WORSHIP IS FRIENDLY

In the Sermon on the Mount, Jesus nailed a common worship problem. He said, "So if you are standing before the altar in the temple, offering a sacrifice to God, and you suddenly remember that someone has something against you, leave your sacrifice there beside the altar. Go and be reconciled to that person. Then come and offer your sacrifice to God" (Matt. 5:23–24).

I saw a cartoon one time that showed a certain congregation from the vantage point of the preacher as he stood in the pulpit. What he saw were all of his church members decked out in battle fatigues with rifles and ammo belts. The members on the right side of the aisle had built a sandbag fortress and were firing and lobbing grenades at the members on the other side, who happened to be rolling a tank in through the side entrance!

It's inevitable that problems will arise between followers of Christ, but they must never be allowed to fester. Otherwise, they will be brought into the church and poison the entire fellowship. Is there someone in your church with whom you're upset right now? Or perhaps you know that someone is upset with you. Please, for the sake of the body of Christ, go immediately to that person and try to make peace. Paul said, "Do your part to live in peace with everyone, as much as possible" (Rom. 12:18).

God Is Pleased When Our Worship Is FRESH

Psalm 33:1–3 says, "Let the godly sing with joy to the Lord, for it is fitting to praise him. Praise the Lord with melodies on the lyre; make music for him on the ten-stringed harp. *Sing new songs of praise to him;* play skillfully on the harp and sing with joy" (author's emphasis). In Scripture, we are commanded to sing new songs, and we're told that new songs will be sung in heaven (Rev. 14:3).

Of course, the point is not that we can't sing old songs when we worship. The point is that we should keep our worship fresh and alive.

But be careful! Don't use this truth as an excuse to bulldoze your brothers and sisters who have more traditional tastes. "Fresh and alive" doesn't necessarily mean totally contemporary. Many congregations have been successful blending the new and the old together, recognizing that the great hymns of the faith are an important part of our heritage, while the newer songs speak effectively to the younger generation. It doesn't have to be an "either/or" situation.

When I was in Bible college, I was told, "Always put out fresh bread. Everybody loves fresh bread." I've tried to apply that advice to music, as well as my preaching and teaching. I believe it's some of the best advice I've ever received.

GOD IS PLEASED WHEN OUR WORSHIP IS FESTIVE

Psalm 135:3 says, "Praise the Lord, for the Lord is good; celebrate his wonderful name with music." Other Scriptures refer to shouting, handclapping, playing musical instruments and even dancing in worship. Clearly, God is pleased when our worship is upbeat and festive. Yes, there should be quiet times of prayer and meditation (Ps. 46:10), but the overall tone of worship should be joyful.

This past week, I met a newcomer to our church who is quite an expressive worshiper. I wouldn't say he dances during the music, but then again, I wouldn't say he doesn't! It's a kind of bouncy little rhythmic hip-hop thing he does with his hands raised high. Okay, he dances. But he isn't annoying, and he doesn't disrupt anybody else's worship experience. As I was chatting with him, he said something interesting: "When I come to worship, I just get so excited. I was diagnosed with cancer a while back, and the doctors told me I would be dead by now. But I sought healing from the Lord and, just look at me. I'm in great shape and I feel fine! God is so good!"

His story reminded me of David's words in Psalm 30:11: "You have turned my mourning into joyful dancing. You have taken away my clothes of mourning and clothed me with joy, that I might sing praises to you and not be silent."

Not every Christian has been healed of cancer, but we've all been saved, and a few have been saved *and* healed. Others have overcome...

deadly addictions,

serious family problems,

financial disaster,

depression,

loneliness,

confusion,

abuse,

and a host of other problems. Doesn't it stand to reason that a gathering of all these people should be an absolute celebration? *Any* worship service should be crowded with people who are so happy and thankful they can hardly stand it!

GOD IS PLEASED WHEN
OUR WORSHIP IS FREQUENT

Psalm 92:1–2 says, "It is good to give thanks to the Lord, to sing praises to the Most High. It is good to proclaim your unfailing love *in the morning,* your faithfulness *in the evening*" (author's emphasis). Obviously, the psalmist is not referring to attending organized corporate worship events that are held twice a day. Rather, he's talking about an attitude of worship that never ends. He's saying that from the time we get up in the morning until we go to bed in the evening, our hearts should be set on the Lord.

I am blessed to have my wife as my secretary and personal assistant. That means I am with her day and night. She's the last person I see when I go to bed, the first person I see when I get up, the first person I see when I get to work, the last person I see when I leave work, and ... well ... you get the idea. Every time I turn around, there she is. But I love it! Why? Because I love *her!* Some people express amazement that we are able to spend so much time together without scratching each other's eyes out. To me, that is so funny. Why *wouldn't* I want to spend a lot of time with my favorite person in the whole world? Even when I'm traveling, we often talk three or four times a day.

The point is, you can't get too much of someone you love with all your heart. When you worship the Lord in spirit and in truth, whether it's in church or in the privacy of your home, you're telling Him you love him. And when you do it frequently, you're telling Him you love Him *a lot.*

*   *   *

One of my favorite worship passages is Micah 6:6–8. Read it carefully:

> *What can we bring to the Lord to make up for what we've done? Should we bow before God with offerings of yearling calves? Should we offer him thousands of rams and tens of thousands of rivers of olive oil? Would that please the Lord? Should we sacrifice our firstborn children to pay for the sins of our souls? Would that make him glad?*
>
> *No, O people, the Lord has already told you what is good, and this is what he requires: to do what is right, to love mercy, and to* walk humbly with your God. *(author's emphasis)*

My friend, it's not the *ritual,* but the *relationship* God desires. Tens of thousands of sacrifices and rivers of olive oil would mean nothing to Him if He couldn't walk with you day by day. So walk with Him. Let Him lead, but walk with Him and worship Him. And when you feel the path turn uphill, as it most certainly will, realize what has happened. It means you've done it.

You've started to climb!

Summit Up: Questions for Personal Reflection or Group Discussion

CHAPTER ONE:
LIFT UP YOUR EYES

1. How old were you when you accepted Christ? At the time, did you understand what you were getting into? Did you expect the Christian life to be easier than it is? Did you live for awhile in the valley of mediocrity? Are you still living there?

2. What triggered your desire to climb? Were you *drawn* or *driven* to the mountain of the Lord? How do you think that motivation has affected you? Has it made you more intense? More urgent? More thankful? More patient? More tolerant of other climbers?

3. Chapter 1 mentions four treasures climbers will find on the mountain of the Lord: people, perspective, potential and peace. Which of these has meant the most to you? Are there other treasures you have discovered? What are they?

4. Altitude changes our perspective. Can you name something you view differently now that you've been climbing awhile?

Chapter Two:
GIRD UP YOUR MIND

1. The Bible teaches that there is a lion prowling the mountain of the Lord (1 Peter 5:8). Have you encountered him? In what ways has he affected your climb? Has his presence forced you to make adjustments in the way you climb?

2. How do you feel about the "What Would Jesus Do?" movement? Do you feel it is merely another example of the commercialization of religion? Or do you think it truly has helped God's people live more righteously?

3. Chapter 2 talks about the importance of quality climbing instruction and guide service. Who was your first spiritual climbing instructor? How did that person influence you? Name one or two of the most important things he/she taught you. Have you ever taught anyone to climb?

4. Abraham, David and Peter all had lapses in judgment. Can you name a time when you made a foolish mistake simply because you weren't thinking? What price did you pay for that mistake?

5. Chapter 2 suggests that worries, walls and weaknesses often keep us from thinking clearly. Which of these gives you the most trouble? What steps have you taken to correct the problem?

CHAPTER THREE:
JOIN UP WITH AN EXPEDITION

1. Some people prefer to climb solo on the mountain of the Lord. What might be the benefits of climbing solo? Why do you think God insists that we climb together?

2. Have you ever been a part of an expedition (church) that you felt was camping instead of climbing? What made you feel that way? How did you react?

3. Does the church you're a part of right now have a vision? If so, can you state it? Do you agree with it? Why? Do you feel your church is accomplishing its vision?

4. In what specific ways do you contribute to the health and growth of your church? If you suddenly died, would your church miss you?

CHAPTER FOUR:
GATHER UP YOUR GEAR

1. Paul mentions the "belt of truth" as being an essential piece of the Christian's climbing gear. Has there ever been a time when you unwittingly believed a lie? What price did you pay? Who finally helped you see the truth?

2. Solomon said, "Above all else, guard your heart, for it affects everything you do" (Prov. 4:23). What are some specific things a Christian can do to guard his heart?

3. The shield of faith is our protection against Satan's projectiles. What are some things Satan has thrown at you? How did your faith help you survive?

4. Think about the condition of your climbing gear right now. Has it deteriorated in recent months or years? Have you grown more susceptible to Satan's attacks? Have you lost ground on the mountain? If so, why? Can you pinpoint a time when you began to lose altitude? What do you need to do to start climbing again?

CHAPTER FIVE:
CLEAN UP YOUR LIFE

1. Chapter 5 shows the difference between Joseph and Samson. Joseph was committed to purity and was blessed, while Samson lived an immoral lifestyle and suffered many problems as a result. Can you name other Bible characters who suffered because of immorality? What about people in our generation? Do you see any common characteristics these individuals share?

2. How have the terrorist attacks of recent years affected the way you live your life? Have they made you more fearful? Angry? Cautious? Suspicious? Do you see any similarities between the terrorists' methods and Satan's methods?

3. Can you think of a time when Satan hit you with a surprise attack? Has he ever tempted you at church or when you have been in the company of your fellow climbers?

4. Have you ever had to perform "spiritual surgery" on yourself (Matt. 5:29–30)? If so, what was it you had to "cut out" and get rid of? Is there something you're clinging to right now that you need to dispose of? Why haven't you done it?

5. How do you react to your own moral failures? Do you trust God's grace to completely remove your sin, or do you wallow in guilt after making a mistake? What does your reaction say to God?

6. Chapter 5 talks about the dangers of legalism, or making purity your *god* rather than your *goal*. Name some of the qualities of a legalist. Do you see any of these in yourself?

CHAPTER SIX:
FIRM UP YOUR COMMITMENT

1. Can you name something you've accomplished in life that was due to sheer commitment? What kept you going? Has it been worth the effort you put in?

2. Chapter 6 talks about how *cynics* and *critics* will try to undermine your commitment. Which of these groups gives you the most trouble? Why?

3. Can you name something specific you have suffered *because* you are a climber on the mountain of the Lord? When that suffering came, did you think about retreating to the valley? What helped you decide what to do?

4. Paul said, "I bear on my body the scars that show I belong to Jesus" (Gal. 6:17b). Can you name some specific signs that show you belong to Jesus?

CHAPTER SEVEN:
BUILD UP YOUR INTEGRITY

1. Rob Hall gave his life to keep his integrity intact. Can you name something you have given up for the sole purpose of protecting your integrity?

2. Are there times when you're not completely honest about who you are? Are there times when you prefer to keep secret the fact that you are a Christian? Have you ever been caught doing something you were ashamed of?

3. Chapter 7 talks about the shining example of NBA star A. C. Green. Can you name someone who has been a great example of integrity to you? Name something specific that person does that impresses you.

4. Whose approval do you crave? Have there been times when you have sought the applause of men over the approval of God? How did you feel afterward?

Chapter Eight:
SOAK UP YOUR BLESSINGS

1. Beck Weathers suffered terribly on Mt. Everest, but in the end he said, "I gained so much more than I lost." How would you evaluate your gains and losses on the mountain of the Lord? Can you name some things you've gained? Some things you've lost?

2. Do you ever feel that you must have a target painted on your chest? Does it sometimes seem that Satan is taking dead aim at you? Are there some parts of your life that have become more difficult since you started climbing?

3. Can you tell about a time of suffering in your life that you were able to endure because you had a *faithful friend* and a *firm foundation?*

4. Chapter 8 maintains that one of the secrets of successful climbing is keeping your eyes on eternity. What are some practical ways you can do that?

Chapter Nine:
OFFER UP YOUR WORSHIP

1. Both David and Jesus had elevated views of worship. What evidence can you point to that proves you have an elevated view of worship?

2. How has your church been affected by the "worship wars" of the last twenty years? Do you feel God is honored when Christians bicker over musical styles and personal preferences?

3. Jesus condemned a lot of very religious people who were temple regulars. To what did Jesus object about these people? Do you see any of those same characteristics in yourself?

4. How often do you come out of a worship service feeling unfulfilled? What are some things you could do to enhance your worship experience? Is it possible that you aren't getting enough out of the service because you aren't putting enough into it?

5. Why do you go to church? To observe certain rituals that have become a part of your routine, or because you value your relationship with God? What evidence is there to prove that you value the relationship more than the rituals?

References

Jeremiah, David, *A Bend in the Road*. Nashville: Word Publishing, 2000.

Russel, Bob, *When God Builds a Church*. West Monroe: Howard Publishing, 2000.

About the Author

Mark Atteberry has been the Senior Minister of Poinciana Christian Church in Kissimmee, Florida, since 1989. He is married to Marilyn, his high-school sweetheart, and is the proud father of one daughter, Michelle. Mark is also an accomplished jazz saxophonist, a collector of fine jazz recordings and an avid sports fan. He loves to hear from his readers and can be contacted through his website, *www.mark atteberry.net.*

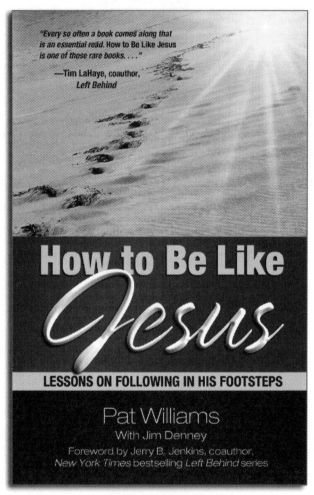

"Every so often a book comes along that is an essential read. How to Be Like Jesus is one of those rare books. . . ."

—Tim LaHaye, coauthor, Left Behind

How to Be Like Jesus

LESSONS ON FOLLOWING IN HIS FOOTSTEPS

Pat Williams
With Jim Denney

Foreword by Jerry B. Jenkins, coauthor,
New York Times bestselling Left Behind series

Code #0693 • Paperback • $14.95

Some books change the way you think; this book could change the way you live.

—Josh McDowell

FINDING the HERO in YOUR HUSBAND

Surrendering the Way God Intended

Dr. Julianna Slattery

WITH AN EXPANDED STUDY GUIDE

Code #2343 • Paperback • $12.95

Stay on God's path with this honest, practical and indispensable book on marriage.